Baseball & The Game of Ideas: Essays for the Serious Fan

BASEBALL & THE GAME OF IDEAS: ESSAYS FOR THE SERIOUS FAN is the second volume in a series on baseball published by Birch Brook Press. The first, edited by Peter C. Bjarkman, was BASEBALL & THE GAME OF LIFE: STORIES FOR THE THINKING FAN.

Baseball & The Game of Ideas: Essays for the Serious Fan

Edited by Peter C. Bjarkman

Thomas L. Altherr * John S. Bowman * Merritt Clifton
Jay Feldman * Bill Fitsell * Stephen Jay Gould
Mark Harris * Dave Healy and Paul Healy
John Hildebidle * John B. Holway * William Humber
James Kissane * David Q. Voigt

Published in the U.S.A. by BIRCH BROOK PRESS
in arrangement with THE SMITH, the distributor

ISBN: 0-913559-19-9
Library of Congress Catalog number: 92-72295

Art by Alfred P. Ingegno, Jr.

Typesetting by Pro•To•Type, Middletown, NY

Printing by Royal Fireworks, Unionville, NY

Binding by Spectrum Bindery, Florida, NY

For a free catalog of books & art, write:

Birch Brook Press
P.O. Box 81
Delhi, NY 13753

THE LINE-UP

For Coach Roger Wickman,
who once let an unskilled but enthusiastic freshman
have his own rare "turn at bat"

INTRODUCTION:
Box Scores & the Music of the Spheres

By PETER C. BJARKMAN

One day I'm going to put all this in a book or a play. I'm going to be a writer like Ring Lardner or somebody—that's if things don't work out first with the Yankees, or the Cubs, or the Red Sox, or maybe possibly the Tigers.... If I get down to the St. Louis Browns, then I'll definitely be a writer.
—*Neil Simon,* Brighton Beach Memoirs

i.

NOT ALL ACADEMICS AND INTELLECTUALS are hopelessly in love with baseball. And not all of them are entirely seduced by the transparent lie that contemporary professional baseball is a perfect metaphor for rosy models of commerce, community, and fair play (rather than a distasteful and exploitive entertainment industry where owners and players are motivated by little beyond the bottom contract line). It may only seem that way, given the recent spate of gushing testimonials. For one mean-spirited commentator, at least, the commonalities between the world of the diamond and the world of the academy draw a less than favorable parallel. Helene Solheim of Bellevue, Washington here proves the antithesis of Roger Angell: "It is no wonder that baseball has a certain appeal to some intellectuals: It is a game in which the action is slow, interminable, and boring; it ties up a lot of expensive real estate to no clear purpose; makes idle, beer-drinking spectators of the masses; is played by committees who dress all alike and not very well, and haven't changed their style in a century; and though a dozen players are on the field at once, only one, or possibly two, are doing anything significant at any one time. . . ."

Writing in the *Chronicle of Higher Education,* Ms. Solheim thus dismisses our national pastime as little more than an ivy-covered sandlot. Of course we could roundly condemn Professor Solheim as a sour academic spoilsport, completely out of touch with the true pulse of the hot dog-eating and beer-drinking American public. Or perhaps, on more careful inspection, we should loudly praise her for that raw tongue-in-cheek prose that colors some of the best of our baseball writing.

I, myself, would prefer to rely more upon the judgments of Walt Whitman, Thomas Wolfe, Marianne Moore, Ernest Hemingway and other men and women of letters who have seen in the national game such huge and resounding metaphors for the meaning of life (baseball = childhood, baseball = frontier spirit, baseball = native American mythology, etc.). Or on those equally intellectual modern-day chroniclers of the game like Roger Angell, Thomas Boswell and Donald Hall, all of whom conclude that baseball is indeed quite profound and meaningful. I opt with Boswell—that time does after all begin on Opening Day and life does imitate the World Series; and apparently scores of doctors, lawyers, professors and Indian chiefs continue to cast a similar ballot.

It seems indisputable, at very least, that baseball is the most memorable of all our national games. Angell tells us that this is quite simply because it is the most carefully watched of all spectator sports. Baseball's classic pacing—innings measured by recorded outs and not a frantically ticking second hand—allows plenty of luxurious space for reflection and analysis. Fans respond between pitches not only to the actions of a moment before, but to layers upon layers of recorded baseball history. Remember when Mays robbed Andy Pafko with a running back-handed stab of a sharp liner in a crucial pennant-race contest of 1955? When Spahn caught Yogi Berra looking at a third strike in game six of the '58 Series? When it was Spahn and Sain and hope that it would rain? Baseball is full of most pleasant ghosts. Each present moment evokes shadows of the happy past.

It is not surprising, then—given baseball's ingrained appeal to memory—that the most passionate debates among fans are those having to do with the existence of a "golden age" lost somewhere in baseball's extensively chronicled past. Weren't the players truly greater in our youth (i.e., the cherished childhood of the reminiscer) than they are today? Can Canseco or Gwynn ever stand comparison with Mantle or Snider? Have there been any durable pitchers of late to match a Spahn or Marichal or Robin Roberts? Was the game somehow sweeter and at the same time more electrifying in the epoch when games were still played in daylight and on real grass? Haven't domes and Astroturf and designated hitters and multi-million-dollar contracts ruined a once pure pastoral game?

Yet despite all the nay-saying about present-day players (.275 hitters with million-dollar paychecks) and conditions (plastic outfields and shopping mall indoor ballparks), it is hard to dispute the health of the national game at the outset of the final decade of the 20th century. Baseball is enjoying an extraordinary boom era of growth and affluence. The players over all certainly seem stronger than ever before, as well—they run faster, hit farther, throw harder, and are generally of hitherto unmatched physical stature. As Stephen Jay Gould will tell us in the pages that follow (in his explication of the demise of the .400 hitter), loss in extremes of performance (.400 averages, sub-2.00 ERAs, Ruthian home run totals) are only a small price to pay for the overall excellence of modern-day play. Some of the fun may be gone, but the pure artistry of diamond play has never been greater. Perhaps we are simply spoiled by the grandness of it all.

One measure of baseball's current sweeping grip upon its adoring public is the amazing phenomenon of baseball literature to which we have been witness over the past two decades. Baseball volumes (histories, biographies, statistical summaries, novels, personal memories of fans and players alike) now seem to line the shelves of local bookstores in nearly the same abundance as timeless sellers like cookbooks, personal growth manuals and "who-done-it" suspense thrillers; each new spring season brings more fresh baseball titles than any devotee of diamond literature could consume in a dozen summers of leisure-time reading (see sections at the end of this volume for our own suggested non-fiction reading list in the field of baseball literature). Hardly a star player or a legendary team or a glorious pennant campaign of the past has not enjoyed its own book-length documentation. There are now almost as many good baseball writers as pennant challengers on Opening Day (William Curran, Roger Angell and Michael Seidel head my own list of Hall-of-Fame candidates); almost as many bad ones as newly minted millionaire players' agents. Each spring brings half a dozen fresh articles in the trade journals about whether or not the boom in baseball books has finally peaked. Yet the very presence of such articles is of itself the most persuasive evidence that such questions must still be answered with a resounding negative.

Two things are most surprising about our baseball books, beyond their mere explosion in numbers. The first is their irrepressible and often relentless intellectual qualities. Certainly our other sports never generate such quality writing, despite Donald Hall's bold contention that generally the best prose these days is likely to be found quite regularly on America's daily newspaper sports pages (cf. Hall 1985). A second puzzling feature of baseball's literature is also directly related to the stark intellectualism of the sport. This is the amount of print that academics of all sorts have devoted to postulating about precisely why baseball, of all our European "bat and ball" games, so steadfastly holds their attention and their interest. Of course, there is a great deal of rationalizing going on here—it is, after all, endless good fun but at the same time professionally embarrassing to be a hopeless fan of mere boys' games. But certainly the evidence is indisputable that writers and thinkers by the library full have taken their mentor Jacques Barzun quite literally ("if you wish to understand America you must first understand baseball") and thus expend considerable energy searching for glimpses of the American psyche within the pageant of the nation's favored pastime.

If one reads widely enough in this discourse provided by the baseball book industry a convergence of opinion seems eventually to emerge. It is not always stated fully in any single source; it is rarely codified simply and all at once by any given writer. But it is indeed possible to make sense out of the nature of baseball's pervasive intellectual appeal. Thus before launching into the fresh collection of essays that follow, some pages might well be devoted here to explicating yet one more time the seemingly essential nature of baseball's unabashed intellectual aura.

ii.

Like the four bases demarcating boundaries of play within the infield of the diamond, baseball's essential appeal seems to consist of four interrelated thematic dimensions. The first might be simplistically labelled as the unrivaled **"humanism"** of the game. Baseball is played by average-sized people (usually men, of course) who repeatedly display their numerous foibles and resulting errors alongside their rare moments of true heroism; it is a game with whose players we can thus intimately identify, and whose glories and disasters appear within equal easy reach of every citizen of the grandstand. And if baseball appeals directly to our sense of identification—our dire need for personal heroes and goats—it also appeals to our deep-rooted human need to codify and to count. For baseball's second appeal is to be found in its built-in **"mathematical aura"** and pervasive statistical flavor. Everything in the game can be—and repeatedly is—counted; all is codified and set down for analysis and interpretation; everything that happens is made permanent by assignment in the game's ever-present record books. And because baseball is so thoroughly recorded, it is a game with an institutionalized depository of memory unrivaled by all other sport. **Memory** (games and heroes recalled from summers past) is indeed baseball's third rich appeal. And finally there is the stark **narrative structure** of the unfolding game itself. Each contest lasting nine innings, each summer's evolving pennant race, the hypnotic cycle of individual ballplaying careers and unfolding seasons, all open before us like the suspenseful tale of a master storyteller.

Baseball "humanness" comes in several intimately related packages. First and foremost is the aforementioned matter of personal identity with our ballplaying heroes. This is a game we all can play—at the country club picnic, on the industrial league softball field, in the backyard or sidestreet with tennis ball and broom handle, and most of all in our delicious daydreams. Or at least it is a game which—unlike football with its bruising hulks and basketball with its oversized acrobatic leapers—gives the deceptive illusion of a contest that even the weak-armed and sloth-footed can master. How else does one explain major leaguers like Wayne Terwilliger or Roy Smalley or Bobby Shantz? It is, of course, all a seductive illusion. (There is in reality no athletic skill more challenging than that of hitting a round ball with a round bat!) But the same citizen who would never dare to face an onrushing NFL lineman or mix it up under the backboards with Charles Barkley would be all too eager to try his luck in the batter's box against the dancing knuckleball of a Charlie Hough or Tom Candiotti.

We understand that this is all deception, even when we mock the error just committed by our favorite major leaguer. None of us could hope to hit a big league curve with a 35-ounce Louisville Slugger; nothing more terrifies than holding one's ground in a batter's box in the face of a ninety-mile-per-hour fastball. The skills of even the most mediocre major league journeyman stretch far beyond our ken. Every fan knows of some local phenom who never got even a moment's look at his one big league try-out camp. But the illusion is subtle—and thus we all grip a bat and clutch a ball, even if the bat is aluminum and the ball is an oversized powderpuff used in a hometown underhand slow-pitch league.

And because professional baseball players appear to be so human, they also are subjected to repeated failures. It is perhaps the most oft-repeated truism of the game (yet still one of the most inscrutable principles) that even the best big leaguers succeed but three of ten tries. A man hitting safely that often is a league all-star (and a millionaire as well by today's pay scales). And since the game is built upon an altar of failure, it is baseball's goats and not its last-second heroes that stand as the sport's most memorable characters. This is indeed the diamond's unique and inexplicable charm. Had Casey of Mudville stroked a titanic homer he would have been forgotten in a day. It would have been the hurler McDuff who gave up that fatal blow to Casey who would now hold a cherished niche in our baseball mythology. Casey (who hopelessly fanned the air with his mighty mis-timed swing) is our true baseball archetype. We remember Fred Merkle who didn't touch second in 1908 and reputedly lost a pennant for the Giants in the process, but not the New York batter whose game-winning safety was suddenly erased by Merkle's folly. Ralph Branca is as much a legendary figure as Bobby Thomson—Ralph Terry as mythic in stature as Bill Mazeroski.

At the other end of the spectrum, of course, baseball has its seemingly larger-than-life heroes. But these are heroes with a debilitating wrinkle. If football's Jim Brown is an iron-clad medieval warrior and basketball's Michael Jordan is a soaring space god, Babe Ruth was a swagging bumpkin in baggy pants, a truly comic figure sporting a pouch on his waistline and a gimp in his home run swagger. And it is to be remembered as well that for generations before television and the modern age of instant celebrities, baseball players were our only true sports heroes—perhaps our only true national heroes. The case may well be made that those diamond demigods of yesteryear (Ruth, Gehrig, DiMaggio, Williams, Feller, Mantle) were also our nation's very last sporting heroes. Today we have only celebrities, such as Jose Canseco, who is as infamous for his fast cars as he is for his home run stroke.

It is the mathematics—the statistics of the game—that codifies this rare balance in baseball between its memorable heroes and its equally memorable goats. Every hit and every error is a recorded part of baseball history. (As Casey Stengel says, in baseball you can always look it up!) No play goes unrecorded and thus few go unremembered. Each individual diamond performer is responsible for each play he executes or doesn't execute, and the record book and the balance sheet we call a box score are entirely unforgiving in this regard. Each player is held fully accountable. Pitchers are measured by their ERA, batters foremost by their hitting and slugging averages, but also by such reality-checks as on-base percentage, runners left in scoring position, strikeouts-per-game ratios, and a host of other yardsticks of daily performance. Try this with football. Fans and commentators alike rarely discern who actually made a block on the interior line which sprung a winning touchdown (or who actually missed a tackle which contributed equally to the same busted play); neither are recorded by any meaningful scoresheet numbers.

It is not just that baseball numbers are meticulously recorded. They are remembered—not just by historians and professional annalists, but by everyday fans to boot. Mention these numbers to any baseball fan—714, .406, 511, 56, 2160, 61, 755, 4192—and spark an immediate heated discussion or witness a knowing smile of recognition. Each is a sacred part of Americana, each springs forth a mythic tale and a flood of heroic memory. There is much more to the game's fascination with numbers, as well, of course. There is, first off, perfection in the geographical and chronological measurements of the diamond and its actions—nine innings, nine players on a side, ninety feet between bases. There is also a profound symbolism in the use of the numbers *three* and *four*—three strikes and four balls, three outfield posts and four infield slots, four basic playing positions (infield, outfield, pitcher and catcher), three outs for the offense and four bases to protect for the defense. And the numbers *three* and *four* do not seem to arise by mere accident or inexplicable convention; they are instead a signal of baseball's deeply metaphysical foundations. As philosopher Roland Garrett tells us, baseball's temporal structure is captured with the number *three*—three strikes for an out, three outs to an inning, usually at least three appearances at bat for each player in a nine-inning contest (cf. Garrett 1976). And if three is the number associated with the offensive (and thus the temporal side of the contest), *four* is the digit which represents defense and thus spatial structure—four bases and four basepaths (which form the square of the infield where most play occurs), the rectangular boxes which house catcher and batter, four balls for a walk, four bases to transverse for a score, etc. There is, indeed, something of pure cosmic magic to be found here.

Because baseball is memory it is also nostalgia. Every true baseball fan savours his or her own private, almost endless list of near mythical baseball heroes, legendary events and action-filled images: Wee Willie Keeler "hittin' em where they ain't" in the game's infant days; the bowlegged yet agile Honus Wagner gobbling up countless grounders in the Pittsburgh infield at the close of the century's first decade; Tinker to Evers to Chance; John McGraw glowering at the opposition from the Giants' dugout; Grover Cleveland Alexander, with his ever ungainly and shambling walk, almost comical in his undersized cap and oversized uniform, striking down Tony Lazzeri in the crucial game of the 1926 World Series; Pepper Martin running wild across the Gas House summers of St. Louis; Daffiness Dodgers stumbling into memorable traffic jams along the basepaths; slight Carl Hubbell of the Giants mowing down an All-Star lineup in New York's Polo Grounds; barrel-chested Hack Wilson exploiting his blacksmith's arms to drive home another Chicago run; Joltin' Joe DiMaggio legging out one more hit during his miraculous streak in 1941; the sweet swing and not-so-sweet disposition of "Teddy Ballgame" Williams; the towering homerun blasts of Adonis-like Mickey Mantle; the pitching mastery of diminutive Whitey Ford; the high-leg mound actions of Boston's Warren Spahn and Frisco's Juan Marichal; the unhittable fall-away delivery of the Cardinals' Bob Gibson; Willie Mays, cap flying, catching up to a towering Vic Wertz drive; the Amazin' Mets led by Gil Hodges and the still more amazing Whiz Kids inspired by Eddie Sawyer; the last-minute long-ball heroics of Bobby Thomson and Bill Mazeroski; Johnny Bench redefining the position of catcher, and Hank Aaron redefining the standards for power-hitting excellence; Pete Rose dropping hit number 4192 into the Cincinnati outfield, then fumbling away the dreams of millions of fans ... the list could be multiplied almost indefinitely.

Finally, baseball infuses writers of fiction and non-fiction with a special passion since it perfectly mirrors the stuff of their own special literary art form. For baseball is essentially the material of narrative structure. Any ballpark contest is itself an ongoing and theoretically endless storyline. A season unfolds like the architecture of an epic tale. There is the early season drama with each hopeful ballclub (cellar dwellers as well as pennant contenders) starting on equal footing; then the slow pace of the unfolding summer's pennant run with one team after another surging and falling in the standings; soon come the long dog-days of late summer which unwrap themselves with their own languid rhythm; and at last there is the climactic tensions of the final stretch run and World Series challenge. And there is also the developing tale of each individual game: pregame batting practice, early inning action, late inning rallies, the long stretch between, played out at its own pace which is unique to each contest, each game ungoverned by the ticking of any relentless time clock. Perhaps, if we are truly lucky, there is even the added drama of extra-innings as well.

Literature itself is built essentially on memory. Childhood is the special garden in which any writer forages for the pure stuff of recollected emotion and recollected experience. And the writer's interest is nearly always focused primarily upon human character. How, then, can baseball—full of memory, linked to childhood, and presenting a colorful cast of human heroes and goats—fail to pique the interest of each and every writer? Certainly it has gripped an inordinate share of our men and women of refined letters. Baseball has produced a flood of decent novels—those by Mark Harris (the Henry Wiggen trilogy), Philip Roth, Bernard Malamud and Eric Rolfe Greenberg have even superseded the narrow genre of sports fiction and become true American classics. Some of our very best fiction writers have displayed a genuine fascination with and devotion to the game—Roth and Thomas Wolfe wrote repeatedly of its emotional hold upon the scenes of their own rural childhoods. Intellectuals of all ilk return again and again to the diamond to gather appropriate metaphors for human experience. And so many men and women of letters have been simply unabashed fans of the home city team and thus of the game itself. Wherever there's an American man or woman of letters, can the ticket stubs and cracker jacks be far behind!

iii.

There is much heated debate about baseball's true founding father. Is it Abner Graves' Colonel Doubleday? Assuredly not! Does true homage belong to New York City bank teller Alexander Cartwright who mapped out a field of play for his Knickerbocker club in neighboring Hoboken in 1845? What about the forgotten organizers of that less often reported rounders match featuring the Beachville club of Ontario, Canada, and held on June 4th of 1838? Of course, it is now common doctrine that baseball as we today know it was the foster child of slow-paced evolution and not at all an instantaneous product of inspired creation. Yet if we want a single founding father, perhaps a solid case might best be made for British emigre Henry Chadwick. Reporting first cricket matches and later "base-ball matches" for the *New York Times,* newspaper man Chadwick admittedly did not calculate the earliest rules of the newly devised American game, nor did he lay out the very first diamond (Cartwright is given the bulk of the credit for these contributions). But he did pioneer important early rule changes (making baseball a more "scientific" contest) and also provided the sport's first printed guidebook. More importantly, he invented baseball's unique tally sheet—the box score. And thus he provided the single element which most made baseball unlike cricket and unlike all other bat and ball games. It is the box score, after all, which is the soul and symbol of everything that is baseball's four-pronged appeal.

The special place of the box score has again been captured by the dean of our hardball writers, Roger Angell. For the non-fan these small numerical ledgers appearing in the morning sports pages are altogether arcane and indecipherable. Yet for the initiated baseball watcher they are the truest source of endless pleasure and information—information with which to organize a summer-long passion. They bring to us details of the events surrounding the players whose fortunes we have followed religiously between April and September. They provide as well—as Angell so delights in telling us—a magical litany of names which is one of baseball's greatest charms. The familiar names which dot each day's box scores have a rhythm and appropriateness not found in even baseball's best fiction—Willie Mays, Duke Snider, Vida Blue, Smead Jolley, Slim Sallee, Urban Shocker, Luscious Easter, Eli Grba, Burleigh Grimes—Dickensian names peopling the baseball landscape which stretch beyond the imaginative daring of even the most bold among contemporary novelists.

But there is even more to the box score than Angell reveals. Its true function and charm is only fully seen against the four appeals of baseball already outlined. For one thing, it is the box score that best reflects baseball's rare human accountability. It is the box score that is the ideal tally sheet for recording the game's magical and perfect balances. Baseball is, after all, designed in a fashion almost identical to the federal system of checks and balances. Michael Novak does not stretch the point when he suggests that "the balance of the game mirrors an intellectual psychic love of equilibrium that is also exemplified in our form of government" (Novak 1988). And the underpinning motive of this balance is an exquisite fairness. The formal record of the box score shows every error, strikeout, wild pitch—nothing is hidden from view, there are no excuses or cover ups, no ambiguities of blame or credit. And the balance sheet must always tally; for every hit registered to a batter, or every score credited to a baserunner, there will be a corresponding deduction against the pitcher who allowed it. Thus our box score also provides ideal reflection of the sport's endless fascination with mathematical minutiae.

A single box score also serves as a flood of memory. While it is not precisely true (as sometimes stated) that an entire game can be reconstructed pitch-by-pitch from this hieroglyphics, yet it is nearly so. This fact is also the reflection, yet again, of baseball's inescapable narrative structure. The trained connoisseur thus reads a box score like a tension-filled and gripping narrative plot—a pulse-wracking thriller, replete with heroes, villains, victims and champions. The flow of the game is recaptured from the line score, its length and pace is read in the columns of hits, errors, runs, strikeouts and walks. Its cast of characters and their individual contributions have precise numerical form.

Angell, as usual, has said it best. If we doubt the mathematical, narrative and aesthetic appeal of this simple yet complex game we need only peruse the box score. Watch the true fans' unwavering allegiance to this tiny acrostic-like puzzle in the daily press, or ponder its full-blown mysteries. Some classic Angell underscores the point: "To the baseball-bitten, it is not only informative, pictorial and gossipy but lovely in aesthetic structure. It represents happenstance and physical flight exactly translated into figures and history. Its totals—batter's credit and pitcher's debit—balance as exactly as those in an accountant's ledger.... This encompassing neatness permits the baseball fan, aided by experience and memory, to extract from a box score the same joy, the same hallucinatory reality, that prickles the scalp of a musician when he glances at a page of his score of 'Don Giovanni' and actually hears bassos and sopranos, woodwinds and violins."

We have suggested here what seem to be some inescapable reasons why writers, especially, and intellectuals of all ilk, more generally, find baseball to hold such a special appeal not found with the nation's time-clock sports. This does not fully answer, of course, why so many have chosen to write so lovingly and persistently about the favored game of their childhood. Perhaps in the end it is a form of compensation. Angell, or Donald Hall, or Roger Kahn—like the rest of us—could probably never hit a fastball or cleanly make a double play pivot at the keystone. Writers like Hall and Mark Harris and Stephen Jay Gould have repeatedly told us as much about their own dismal ballplaying youth. But once having discovered their poet's art and found legitimacy in the world of academic letters, each soon discovered the fact that these newfound literary talents could once again make them a part of the game, and indeed make the game something of their own possession. We writers are all a bit like Malamud's intrepid sportswriter Max Mercy, who replies to Roy Hobbs' condemning question ("Max, did you ever play the game?") with a cocky affirmation. "No," counters Max, "but I make it a lot more interesting to watch!"

This is, in the end, the achievement and pride of any of us who have ever tried to capture a small piece of this most perfect game on paper or in print. Writers represented in this current volume have thus together addressed each of the special appeals that make baseball so enticing to the American intellectual, and to the casual fan as well. Love or reject any of the following individual pieces. But be forewarned that each is guaranteed to make you think somewhat more deeply about the game which is our shared national passion.

Certain of these essays will stimulate debate about the game's murky origins. William Humber and John Bowman provide contrasting approaches—one scholarly and the other largely playful—to the much debated topic of Abner Doubleday's misty antecedents. Others raise serious question about the game's redeeming social value as entertainment spectacle and model for instructive play. Merritt Clifton and Jay Feldman, for example, take on the positives and negatives of youthful participation in adult-driven organized forms of the national sport. John Hildebidle explores the game's intellectual roots along lines of reasoning that echo yet amplify those implanted in this present essay. Hildebidle, especially, champions the thesis that the excitement of baseball lies mainly in the forces of memory and imagination. David Voigt and John Holway explore as well the lighter veins of baseball history—one looking at off-color characters and the other at pseudo-science employed in the service of performance evaluation. Bill Fitsell and the Healys (Dave and Paul) reexamine the mythic underpinnings of the game's familiar lore, on the one hand, and its obtuse symbolic structures, on the other.

The role of baseball fiction in shaping the game's mythology finds its treatment here from a practicing literary critic as well as from one of the game's pathfinding novelists. Thomas Altherr explores the religious parallels found in the popular fiction of W.P. Kinsella ("Baseball is the one single thing the white man has done right..."). Mark Harris (progenitor of the Henry Wiggen tetrology) traces the roots of his own work to that of Ring Lardner, as well as to plots of boys' dime-novels by masters of pulp fiction like William Heyliger, Harold Sherman, Edward Stratemeyer, Gilbert Patten (a.k.a. Burt L. Standish), John R. Tunis, Ralph Henry Barbour and Zane Grey. Harris here reveals something of precisely why there was such a long embryonic period for the serious adult baseball novel.

Finally, Stephen Jay Gould and James Kissane employ widely diverging methodologies to tackle head on the issue of baseball's evolving and often subtly shifting appearances. In a unique piece, authored two long decades ago, Kissane laments changes altogether familiar to current fans, but ones that were already dismaying ballpark patrons almost a full generation ago. Gould, in turn, brings his familiar flawless reasoning and respected scientific expertise to bear in building an airtight defense for the quality of modern-day play. The notion of a "golden age" when the hitters were stouter and the hurlers more masterful is a mere myth in itself, Gould duly warns. Players may no longer scale Mount Olympus, but larger numbers of the game's denizens than ever before perform at levels unrivaled in previous decades. If we have few or no Ruths or Cobbs, we have no Wayne Terwilligers or Carlos Paulas either. Gould begs us not to lament the loss of seemingly miraculous performance, which is only in reality a measure of the larger failings of ordinary performers; instead we are urged to celebrate the immense improvement in average play that is the standard for today's state-of-the-art game. For us baseball fans this should be easy enough to swallow. For what game, indeed, better notices its average performances, records their every detail, finds poetry and nobility in the routine and the totally commonplace?

In the end all of our authors leave us contemplating Roger Angell's witty aphorism. It seems, indeed, that baseball may well have—somewhere along yesterday's time line of new world political and social evolution—been fortuitously invented just to remind us of all other things in life. Things like our lost childhoods, and like our endlessly repeated emotional trips through the travails of our own private basepaths, in hopeless search for a misplaced route leading back home. It is a grand game, a thinking man's game, and a thinking woman's game as well. It is a game which surely does not mean half of the things we take it to mean. Then again, it probably means so much more. If you doubt me on this point, dear reader, simply open this volume to almost any random page, and contemplate the pure magic of the box score.

References Cited

Angell, Roger. *The Summer Game.* New York: The Viking Press, 1972 (New York: Ballantine Books, 1984).

Boswell, Thomas. *How Life Imitates the World Series.* Garden City, New York: Doubleday and Company, 1982.

Boswell, Thomas. *Why Time Begins on Opening Day.* Garden City, New York: Doubleday and Company, 1984.

Garrett, Roland. "The Metaphysics of Baseball" in: *Philosophy Today* 20 (1976), 209-225.

Hall, Donald. *Fathers Playing Catch With Sons – Essays on Sport [Mostly Baseball].* San Francisco: North Point Press, 1985.

Novak, Michael. *The Joy of Sports – End Zones, Bases, Baskets, Balls, and the Consecration of the American Spirit.* New York: Hamilton Press, 1988.

Why No One Hits .400 Any More

By STEPHEN JAY GOULD

COMPARISONS MAY BE ODIOUS, but we cannot avoid them in a world that prizes excellence and yearns to know whether current pathways lead to progress or destruction. We are driven to contrast past with present and use the result to predict an uncertain future. But how can we make fair comparison since we gaze backward through the rose-colored lenses of our most powerful myth—the idea of a former golden age?

Nostalgia for an unknown past can elevate hovels to castles, dung heaps to snow-clad peaks. I had always conceived Calvary, the site of Christ's martyrdom, as a lofty mountain, covered with foliage and located far from the hustle and bustle of Jerusalem. But I stood on its paltry peak not long ago. Calvary lies inside the walls of old Jerusalem (just barely beyond the city borders of Christ's time). The great hill is but one staircase high; its summit lies *within* the Church of the Holy Sepulchre.

I had long read of Ragusa, the great maritime power of the medieval Adriatic. I viewed it at grand scale in my mind's eye, a vast fleet balancing the powers of Islam and Christendom, sending forth its elite to the vanguard of the "invincible" Spanish Armada. Medieval Ragusa has survived intact—as Dubrovnik in Yugoslavia. No town (but Jerusalem) can match its charm, but I circled the battlements of its city walls in 15 minutes. Ragusa, by modern standards, is a modest village at most.

The world is so much bigger now, so much faster, so much more complex. Must our myths of ancient heroes expire on this altar of technological progress? We might dismiss our deep-seated tendency to aggrandize older heroes as mere sentimentalism—and plainly false by the argument just presented for Calvary and Ragusa. And yet, numbers proclaim a sense of truth in our persistent image of past giants as literally outstanding. Their legitimate claims are relative, not absolute. Great cities of the past may be villages today, and Goliath would barely qualify for the NBA. But, compared with modern counterparts, our legendary heroes often soar much farther above their own contemporaries. The distance between commonplace and extraordinary has contracted dramatically in field after field.

Baseball provides my favorite examples. Our national pastime may strike readers as an odd topic for serious scientific discussion, but few systems offer better data for a scientific problem that evokes as much interest, and sparks as much debate, as any other: the meaning of trends in history as expressed by measurable differences between past and present. How can we compare an elusive past with a different present? How can we know whether past deeds matched or exceeded current prowess? In particular, was Moses right in his early pronouncement (Genesis 6:4): "There were giants in the earth in those days"?

Baseball has been a bastion of constancy in a tumultuously changing world, a contest waged to the same purpose and with the same basic rules for 100 years. It has also generated an unparalleled flood of hard numbers about achievement, measured every which way that human cleverness can devise. Most other systems have changed so profoundly that we cannot meaningfully mix the numbers of past and present. How can we compare the antics of Larry Bird with basketball as played before the 24-second rule or, going further back, the center jump after every basket, the two-hand dribble, and finally nine-man teams tossing a lopsided ball into Dr. Naismith's peach basket? Yet while styles of play and dimensions of ball parks have altered substantially, baseball today is the same game that Wee Willie Keeler and Nap Lajoie played in the 1890s.

Bill James, our premier guru of baseball stats, writes that "the rules attained essentially their modern form after 1893" (when the pitching mound retreated to its current distance of 60 feet 6 inches). The numbers of baseball can be compared meaningfully for a century of play.

When we contrast these numbers of past and present, we encounter the well-known and curious phenomenon that inspired these musings: Great players of the past often stand further apart from their teammates. Consider only the principal measures of hitting and pitching: batting average and earned run average. No one has hit .400 since Ted Williams reached .406 over half a century ago in 1941; yet eight players exceeded .410 in the 50 years before then. Bob Gibson had an earned run average of 1.12 in 1968. Ten other pitchers have achieved a single season E.R.A. below 1.30, but before Gibson we must go back a full 50 years to Walter Johnson's 1.27 in 1918. Could the myths be true after all? Were the old guys really better? Are we heading towards entropic homogeneity and robotic sameness?

These past achievements are paradoxical because we know perfectly well that all historical trends point to a near assurance that modern athletes must be better than their predecessors. Training has become an industry and an obsession, an upscale profession filled with engineers of body and equipment, and a separate branch of medicine has sprung up for the ills of excessive zeal. Few men now make it to the majors just by tossing balls against a barn door during their youth. We live better, eat better, provide more opportunity across all social classes. Moreover, the pool of potential recruits has increased five fold in 100 years by simple growth of the American population.

Numbers affirm this ineluctable improvement for sports that run against the absolute standard of a clock. The Olympian powers-that-be finally allowed women to run the marathon in 1984. Joan Benoit won it in 2:24:54. In 1896, Spiridon Loues had won in just a minute under three hours; Benoit ran faster than any male Olympic champion until Emil Zatopek's victory at 2:23:03 in 1952. Or consider two of America's greatest swimmers of the 1920s and '30s, men later recruited to play Tarzan (and faring far better than Mark Spitz in his abortive commercial career). Johnny Weissmuller won the 100-meter freestyle in 59.0 in 1924 and 58.6 in 1928. The women's record then stood at 1:12.4 and 1:11.0, but Jane had bested Tarzan by 1972 and the women's record has now been lowered to 54.79. Weissmuller also won the 400-meter freestyle in 5:04.2 in 1924, but Buster Crabbe had cut off more than 15 seconds by 1932 (4:48.4). Female champions in those years swam the distance in 6:02.2 and 5:28.5. The women beat Johnny in 1956, Buster in 1964, and by 1984 reached 4:07.10, half a minute quicker than Crabbe.

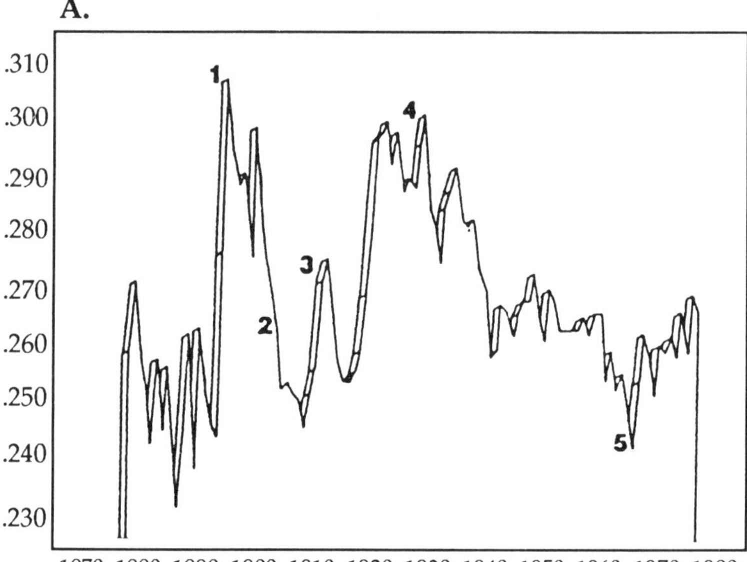

MEAN BATTING AVERAGE BY YEAR

Averages rose after the pitching mound was moved back (1); declined after adoption of the foul-strike rule (2); rose again after the invention of the cork-center ball (3) and during the "lively ball" era (4). The dip in the '60s (5) was "corrected" in 1969 by lowering the pitching mound and decreasing the strike zone.

Baseball, by comparison, pits batter against pitcher and neither against a constant clock. If everyone improves as the general stature of athletes rises, then why do we note any trends at all in baseball records? Why do the best old-timers stand out above their modern counterparts? Why don't hitting and pitching continue to balance?

The disappearance of .400 hitting becomes even more puzzling when we recognize that *average* batting has remained relatively stable since the beginning of modern baseball in 1876. Chart A displays the history of mean batting averages since 1876. (We only included men with an average of at least two at-bats per game since we wish to gauge trends of regular players. Nineteenth-century figures [National League only] include 80 to 100 players for most years [a low of 54 to a high of 147]. The American League began in 1901 and raised the average to 175 players or so during the long reign of two eight-team leagues, and to above 300 for more recent divisional play.) Note the constancy of mean values: The average ballplayer hit about .260 in the 1870s, and he hits about .260 today. Moreover, this stability has been actively promoted by judicious modifications in rules whenever hitting or pitching threatened to gain the upper hand and provoke a runaway trend of batting averages either up or down. Consider all the major fluctuations:

After beginning around .260, averages began to drift downwards, reaching the .240s during the late 1880s and early 1890s. Then, during the 1893 season, the pitching mound was moved back to its current 60 feet 6 inches from home plate (it had begun at 45 feet, with pitchers delivering the ball underhand, and had moved steadily back during baseball's early days). The mean soared to its all-time high of .307 in 1894 and remained high (too high, by my argument) until 1901, when adoption of the foul-strike rule promoted a rapid down-turn. (Previously, foul balls hadn't influenced the count.) But averages went down too far during the 1900s until the introduction of the cork-center ball sent them abruptly up in 1911. Pitchers accommodated, and within two years, averages returned to their .260 level—until Babe Ruth wreaked personal havoc upon the game by belting 29 homers in 1919 (more than entire teams had hit many times before). Threatened by the Black Sox scandal, and buoyed by the Babe's performance (and the public's obvious delight in his free-swinging style), the moguls introduced—whether by conscious collusion or simple acquiescence we do not know—the greatest of all changes in 1920. Scrappy one-run, savvy-baserunning, pitcher's baseball was out; big offense and swinging for the fences was in. Averages rose sharply, and this time they stayed high for a full 20 years, even breaking .300 for the second (and only other) time in 1930. Then in the early 1940s, after war had siphoned off the best players, averages declined again to their traditional .260 level.

The causes behind this 20-year excursion have provoked one of the greatest unresolved debates in baseball history. Conventional wisdom attributes these rises to the introduction of a "lively ball." But Bill James, in his masterly *Historical Baseball Abstract*, argues that no major fiddling with baseballs in 1920 can be proved. He attributes the rise to coordinated changes in rules (and pervasive alteration of attitudes) that imposed multiple and simultaneous impediments upon pitching, upsetting the traditional balance for a full 20 years. Trick pitches—the spitball, shine ball, and emery ball—were all banned. More important, umpires now supplied shiny new balls any time the slightest scruff or spot appeared. Previously, soft, scratched, and darkened balls remained in play as long as possible (fans were even expected to throw back "souvenir" fouls). The replacement of discolored and scratched with shiny and new, according to James, would be just as effective for improving hitting as any mythical "lively ball." In any case, averages returned to the .260s by the 1940s and remained quite stable until their marked decline in the mid-1960s. When Carl Yastrzemski won the American League batting title with a paltry .301 in 1968, the time for redress had come again. The moguls lowered the mound, restricted the strike zone, and averages promptly rose again—right back to their time-honored .260 level, where they have remained ever since.

This exegetical detail shows how baseball has been maintained, carefully and consistently, in unchanging balance since its inception. Is it not, then, all the more puzzling that downward trends in best performances go hand in hand with constancy of average achievement? Why, to choose the premier example, has .400 hitting disappeared, and what does this erasure teach us about the nature of trends and the differences between past and present?

We can now finally explicate the myth of ancient heroes—or, rather, we can understand its partial truth. Consider the two ingredients of our puzzle and paradox: (1) admitting the profound and general improvement of athletes (as measured in clock sports with absolute standards), star baseball players of the past probably didn't match today's leaders (or, at least, weren't notably better); (2) nonetheless, top baseball performances have declined while averages are actively maintained at a fairly constant level. In short, the old-timers did soar farther above their contemporaries, but must have been worse (or at least no better) than modern leaders. The .400 hitters of old were relatively better, but absolutely worse (or equal).

How can we get a numerical handle on this trend? I've argued several times in various articles that students of biological evolution (I am one) approach the world with a vision different from time-honored Western perspectives. Our general culture still remains bound to its Platonic heritage of pigeonholes and essences. We divide the world into a set of definite "things" and view variation and subtle shadings as nuisances that block the distinctness of real entities. At best, variation becomes a device for calculating an average value seen as a proper estimate of the true thing itself. But variation *is* the irreducible reality; nature provides nothing else. Averages are often meaningless (mean height of a family with parents and young children). There is no quintessential human being—only black folks, white folks, skinny people, little people, Manute Bol and Eddie Gaedel. Copious and continuous variation is us.

The necessary item for this study is practical, not ideological. The tools for resolving the paradox of ancient heroes lie in the direct study of variation, not in exclusive attention to stellar achievements. We've failed to grasp this simple solution because we don't view variation as reality itself, and therefore don't usually study it directly.

I can now state, in a few sentences, my theory about trends in general and .400 hitting in particular (sorry for the long cranking up, and the slow revving down to come, but simple ideas with unconventional contexts require some exposition if they hope to become reader-friendly). Athletes have gotten better (the world in general has become bigger, faster, and more efficient—this may not be a good thing at all; I merely point out that it has happened). We resist this evident trend by taking refuge in the myth of ancient heroes. The myth can be exploded directly for sports with absolute clock standards. In a system with relative standards (person against person)—especially when rules are subtly adjusted to maintain constancy in measures of average performance—this general improvement is masked and cannot be recovered when we follow our usual traditions and interpret figures for average performances as measures of real things. We can, however, grasp the general improvement of systems with relative standards by a direct study of variation—recognizing that variation itself is the irreducible reality. This improvement manifests itself as a *decline in variation*. Paradoxically, this decline produces a decrease in the difference between average and stellar performance. Therefore, modern leaders don't stand so far above their contemporaries. The "myth" of ancient heroes—the greater distance between average and best in the past—actually records the improvement of play through time.

Declining variation is the key to our puzzle. Hitting .400 isn't a thing in itself, but an extreme value in the distribution of batting averages (I shall present the data for this contention shortly). As variation shrinks around a constant mean batting average, .400 hitting disappears. It is, I think, as simple as that.

Reason One for Declining Variation: *Approach to the outer limits of human capacity.*

Well-off people in developed nations are getting taller and living longer, but the trend won't go on forever. All creatures have outer limits set by evolutionary histories. We're already witnessing the approach to limits in many areas. Maximum life span isn't increasing (although more and more people live long enough to get a crack at the unchanging heights). Race horses have hardly speeded up, despite the enormous efforts of breeders and the unparalleled economic incentive for shaving even a second off top performance (Kentucky Derby winners averaged 2:06.4 during the 1910s and 2:02.0 for the past ten years). Increase in human height has finally begun to level off (daughters of Radcliffe women are now no taller than their mothers). Women's sports records are

B. THE EXTINCTION OF .400 HITTING

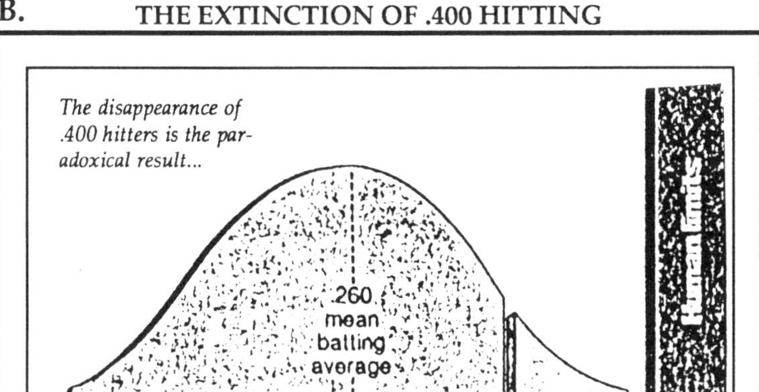

C.

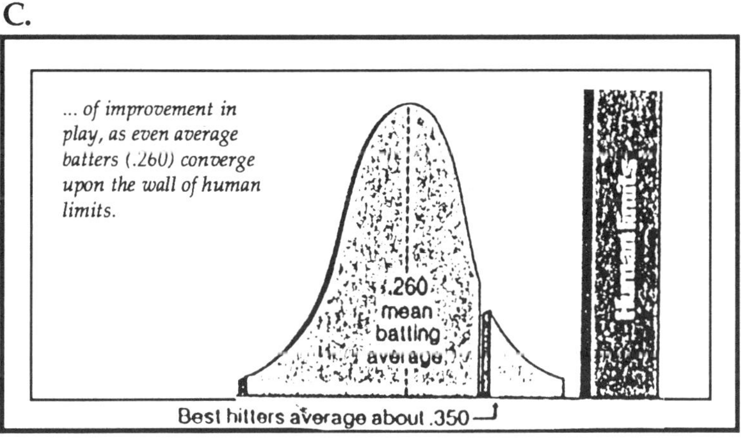

declining rapidly as opportunity opens up, but some male records are stabilizing.

We can assess all these trends, and the inevitable decline in improvement as we reach the outer limits, because they're measured by absolute clock standards. Baseball players must also be improving, but the relative standard of batting averages, maintained at a mean of about .260, masks the advance. Let's assume that the wall at the right in diagram B represents the outer limit, and the bell-shaped curve well to its left marks variation in batting prowess 100 years ago. I suspect that all eras boast a few extraordinary individuals, people near the limits of body and endurance, however lower the general average. So, a few players resided near the right wall in 1880—but the average Joe stood far to their left, and variation among all players was great. Since then, everyone has improved. The best may have inched a bit towards the right wall, but average players have moved substantially in that direction. Meanwhile, increasing competition and higher standards have eliminated very weak hitters (once tolerated for their superior fielding and other skills).

So, as average players approach the limiting right wall (diagram C), variation decreases strongly on both flanks—at the high end for simple decline in space between the average and the limit, and at the low end by decreasing tolerance as general play improves. The relative standards of baseball have masked this trend; hitting has greatly improved, but we still measure its average as .260 because pitching has gained in concert. We can, however, assess this improvement in a different way—by inevitable decline in variation as the average converges upon the limiting wall. Modern stars may be an inch or two closer to the wall—they're absolutely better (or at least no worse) than ancient heroes. But the average has moved several feet closer—and the distance between ordinary (kept at .260) and best has decreased. In short, no more .400 hitters. Ironically, the disappearance of .400 hitting is a sign of improvement, not decline.

Reason Two (really the same point stated differently): *Systems equilibrate as they improve.*

D.

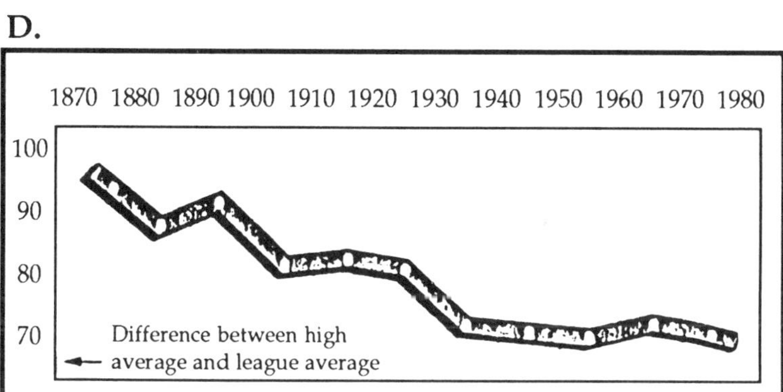

E.

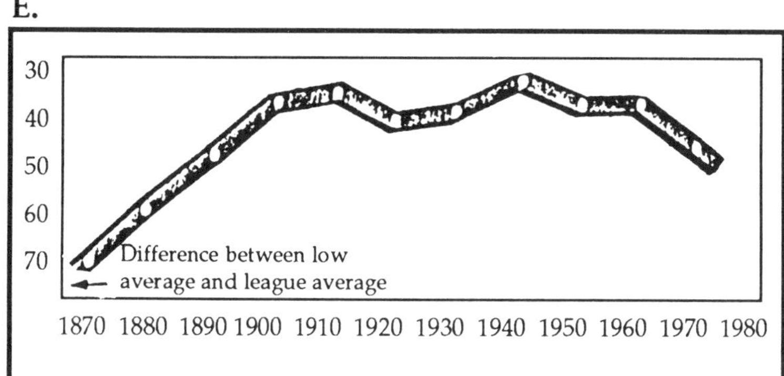

THE DECLINE IN EXTREMES

Batting averages are neither as high nor as low as they used to be.

Baseball was feeling its way during the early days of major league play. Its rules were our rules, but scores of subtleties hadn't yet been developed or discovered; rough edges careered out in all directions from a stable center. To cite just a few examples (again from Bill James): Pitchers began to cover first base in the 1890s; during the same decade, Brooklyn invented the cut-off play, while the Boston Beaneaters developed the hit-and-run and signals from runner to batter. Gloves were a joke in those early days—just a little leather over the hand, not a basket for trapping balls. In 1896 the Phillies actually experimented for 73 games with a lefty shortstop. Traditional wisdom applied. He stank; he had the worst fielding average and the fewest assists in the league among regular shortstops.

In an era of such experiment and indifference, truly great players could take advantage in ways foreclosed ever since. As I wrote in a previous article (*Vanity Fair*, March 1983), Wee Willie Keeler could "hit 'em where they ain't" (and bat .432 in 1897) because fielders didn't yet know where they should be. Consider the predicament of a modern Wade Boggs or a Rod Carew. Every pitch is charted, every hit mapped to the nearest square inch. Fielding and relaying have improved dramatically. Boggs and Keeler probably stood in the same place, just a few inches from the right wall of human limits, but average play has so crept up on Boggs that he lacks the space for taking advantage of suboptimality in others. All these improvements must rob great batters of 10 or 20 hits a year—more than enough to convert our modern best into .400 hitters.

To summarize, variation in batting averages must decrease as improving play eliminates the rough edges that great players could exploit, and as average performance moves towards the limits of human possibility and compresses great players into an ever decreasing space between average play and the unmovable right wall.

I measured this decline of variation about a constant average on the cheap. I simply took the five highest and five lowest averages for regular players in each year and compared them with the league average. I found that differences between both average and highest and between average and lowest have decreased steadily through the years (*see chart D*). The disappearance of .400 hitting—the most discussed and disputed trend in the history of baseball—isn't a reflection of generally higher averages in the past (for no one hit over .400 during the second decade of exalted averages, from 1931 to 1940, and most .400 hitting in our century occurred between 1900 and 1920, when averages stood at their canonical [and current] .260

F.

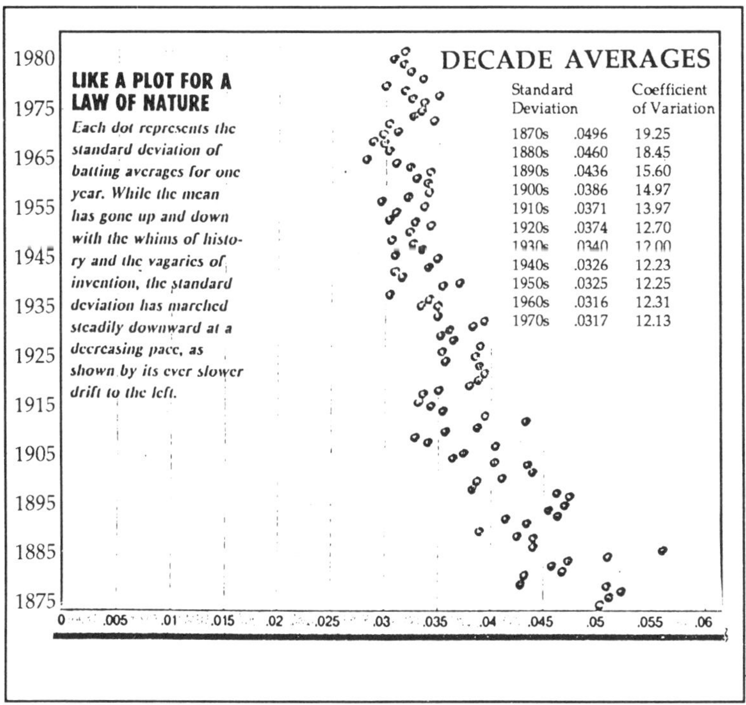

level). Nor can this eclipse of high hitting be entirely attributed to the panoply of conventional explanations that view .400 averages as a former "thing" now extinct—more grueling schedules, too many night games, invention of the slider, better fielding, and relief pitching. For .400 hitting isn't a thing to be extirpated, but an extreme value in a distribution of variation for batting averages. The reasons for declining variation, as presented above, are different from the causes for disappearance of an entity. Declining variation is a general property of systems that stabilize and improve while maintaining constant rules of performance through time. The extinction of .400 hitting is, paradoxically, a mark of increasingly *better* play.

We have now calculated the decline of variation properly, and at vastly more labor (with thanks to my research assistant Ned Young for weeks of work, and to Ed Purcell, Nobel laureate and one of the world's great physicists—but also just a fan with good ideas). The standard deviation is a statistician's basic measure of variation. To compute the standard deviation, you take (in this case) each individual batting average and subtract from it the league average for that year. You then square each value (multiply it by itself) in order to eliminate negative numbers for batting averages below the mean (a negative times a negative gives a positive number). You then add up all these values and divide them by the total number of players—giving an average squared deviation of individual players from the mean. Finally, you take the square root of this number to obtain the average, or standard, deviation itself. The higher the value, the more extensive, or spread out, the variation.

We calculated the standard deviation of batting averages for each year (an improvement from my former high and low five, but much more work). Chart F plots the trend of standard deviations in batting averages year by year. Our hypothesis is clearly confirmed. Standard deviations have been dropping steadily and irreversibly. The decline itself has decelerated over the years as baseball stabilizes—rapidly during the nineteenth century, more slowly through the twentieth, and reaching a stable plateau by about 1940.

If I may make a personal and subjective comment, I was stunned and delighted (beyond all measure) by the elegance and clarity of this result. I pretty well knew what the general pattern would be because standard deviations are so strongly influenced by extreme values (a consequence of squaring each individual deviation in the calculation)—so my original cheap method of five highest and lowest produced a fair estimate. But I never dreamed that the decline would be so regular, so devoid of exception or anomaly for even a single year—so unvarying that we could even pick out such subtleties as the deceleration in decline. I've spent my entire professional career studying such statistical distributions, and I know how rarely one obtains such clean results in better behaved data of controlled experiments or natural growth in simple systems.

We usually encounter some glitch, some anomaly, some funny years. But the decline of standard deviation for batting averages is so regular that it looks like a plot for a law of nature. I find this all the more remarkable because the graph of averages themselves through time (Chart A) shows all the noise and fluctuation expected in natural systems. Yet mean batting averages have been constantly manipulated by the moguls of baseball to maintain a general constancy, while no one has tried to monkey with the standard deviation. Thus, while mean batting averages have gone up and down to follow the whims of history and the vagaries of invention, the standard deviation has marched steadily down at a decreasing pace, apparently perturbed by nothing of note. I regard this regularity of decline as further evidence that decreasing variation through time is the primary predictable feature of stabilizing systems.

The details are impressive in their regularity. All four beginning years of the 1870s sport high values of standard deviation greater than 0.050, while the last reading in excess of 0.050 occurs in 1886. Values between 0.04 and 0.05 mark the rest of the nineteenth century, with three years just below, at 0.038 to 0.040. The last reading in excess of 0.040 occurs in 1911. Subsequently, decline within the 0.03 and 0.04 range shows the same precision of detail by even decrease with years. The last reading as high as 0.037 occurs in 1937, and of 0.035 in 1941. Only two years have exceeded 0.034 since 1957. Between 1942 and 1980, values remained entirely within the restricted range of 0.0285 to 0.0348. I'd thought that at least one unusual year would upset the pattern—that one nineteenth-century value would achieve late twentieth-century lows, or one more recent year soar to ancient highs—but we find no such thing. All measures from 1906 back to the beginning are higher than every reading from 1938 to 1980. We find no overlap at all. This—take it from an old trooper—is regularity with a vengeance. Something general is going on here, and I think I know what.

The decadal averages are listed in Chart F, and show continuous decline before stabilization in the 1940s. (A note for statistically minded readers: Standard deviations are expressed in their own units of measurement—mouse tails in millimeters, mountains in megatons. Thus, as mean values rise and fall, standard deviations may go up and down to track the mean rather than record exclusively the amount of spread. This poses no problem for most of our chart, because averages have been so stable through time at about .260. But the 20-point rise in averages during the 1920s and 1930s might entail artificially elevated standard deviations. We can correct for this effect by computing the coefficient of variation—100 times the standard deviation divided by the mean—for each year. Also listed are decadal averages for coefficients of variation—and we now see that apparent stabilization between the 1910s and 1920s was masking a continuing decline in coefficient of variation, as the 1920s rise in averages canceled out decline in variation when measured by the standard deviation.)

Just one final hint of a more interesting pattern revealed by finer dissection: Chart F amalgamates the two leagues, but their trends are somewhat different. In the National League, variation declined during the nineteenth century, but stabilized early in the twentieth. In the American League, founded in 1901, variation dropped steadily right through the 1940s. Thus, each league followed the same pattern—time of origin setting pattern of decline for decades to come. Can we use existence or stabilization of declining variation as a mark of maturity? Did the leagues differ fundamentally during the early years of our century—the National already mature, the American still facing a few decades of honing and trimming the edges?

No one has invested more time and energy in the study of numbers than baseball aficionados. We have measures and indices for everything imaginable—from simple lists of at-bats to number of times a black shortstop under six feet tall has been caught stealing third on pitchouts by righties to left-handed catchers. Yet I don't think that this most basic pattern in the standard deviation of batting averages has been properly noted, or its significance assessed. As I argued above, the biases of our upbringing force a focus on averages treated as things, and virtually preclude proper attention to variation considered as irreducible reality. The standard deviation is our base-level tool for studying variation—as fundamental as milk for babies and cockroaches for New York apartments. Yet, after decades of loving attention to minutiae of averages, we can still gain insights from an unexplored pattern in the very simplest kiddie measure of variation. What better illustration for my claim that our culture undervalues variation at its peril?

The message of this study in variation might seem glum, almost cosmically depressing in its paradox—that general improvement clips the wings of true greatness. No one soars above the commonplace any more. General advance brings declining variation in its wake; heroes are extinct. The small population of Europe yielded both a Bach and a Mozart in just 100 years; where shall we find such transcendent geniuses to guide (or at least enlighten) our uncertain and perilous present?

I wish to propose a more general framework for understanding trends in time as an interaction between the location of bell-shaped curves in variation and the position (and potential for mobility) of the limiting right wall for human excellence. This theme transcends sports (or any particular example), and our model should include mind work as well as body work. I suggest three rough categories, with a fundamental example for each, ranging from high to low potential for future accomplishment.

Consider science as a system of knowledge. In most areas, our ignorance is abysmal compared with our sense of what we might learn and know. The curve of knowledge, in other words, stands far from the right wall. Moreover, the wall itself (or at least our perception of it) seems flexible before the growth of knowledge, as new theories suggest pathways to insight never considered previously. Science seems progressive since current ignorance provides so much space to its right, and since the wall itself can be pushed back by the very process that signals our approach. Still, one cannot avoid—with that special sadness reserved for recognizing a wonderful thing gone forever—the conviction that certain seminal discoveries established truths so central and so broad in import that we cannot hope to win insight in such great gulps again, for the right wall moves slowly and with limits, and we may never again open up space for jumps so big. Plate tectonics has revolutionized geology, but we cannot match the thrill of those who discovered that time comes in billions, not thousands—for deep time, once discovered, set the root of a profession forever. These are exciting days for biology, but no one will taste the intellectual power of a man alone at Downe—Charles Darwin reformulating all nature with the passkey of evolution.

I would place most sports, as well as musical performance, in a second category, where the best have long stood near an inflexible right wall. When we remove impediments imposed by custom (women's sports) or technology (certain musical instruments), improvement may be rapid. But progress comes in inches or milliseconds for goals long sought and unimpeded (I doubt that Stern plays notably better than Paganini, Horowitz than Liszt, E. Power Biggs than Bach—and neither horse nor human male is shaving much off the mile run these days). The small contribution of this essay lies in this second domain—in showing that decline in variation will measure improvement when relative standards mask progress measured against such absolute criteria as clocks.

Lest we lament this second category for its limited licenses in improvement, consider the painful plight of a third domain where success in striving depletes the system itself. The right wall of our first domain was far away and somewhat flexible, near and rigid (but still stable) in our second. In this third domain, success hits the wall and consumes it—as if the mile run had disappeared as a competitive sport as soon as 100 people ran the distance in less than four minutes. Given an ethic that exalts perennial originality in artistic composition, the history of music (and many other arts) may fall into this domain. One composer may exploit a basic style for much of a career, but successors may not follow this style in much detail, or for very long. Such striving for newness may grant us joy forever if a limitless array of potential styles awaits discovery and exploitation. But perhaps the world is not so bounteous; perhaps we've already explored most of what even a highly sophisticated audience can deem accessible. Perhaps the wall of an intelligible vanguard has been largely consumed. Perhaps there is a simple solution to the paradox of why we now generate no Bach or Mozart in a world far larger, with musical training provided for millions more. Perhaps they reside among us, but we've consumed all styles of expression so deeply tuned to the human soul. If so, I might timidly advance a truly reactionary proposal. The death of Mozart at 35 may have been the deepest tragedy of our cultural history (great scientists have died even younger, but their work can be done by others). We perform his handful of operas over and over again. We might be enjoying a dozen more—some counted as the most sublime of all musical works—if he had survived even to 50. Suppose a composer now lived who could master his style and write every bit as well. The ethic of originality forbids it absolutely, but would the integrity of art collapse forever if this person wrote just a few more great pieces in that genre? Not a hundred, just three or four to supplement *Don Giovanni* and *Die Zauberflöte*. Would this not be esteemed a public service beyond all others?

I'm waxing lugubrious, despite promises to the contrary. For while I may yearn to hear Beethoven's tenth symphony, I don't lament a lost past or decry a soft present. In sport, and art, and science (how I wish it were so in politics as well), we live in the best world we've ever known, though not in the best of all possible worlds. So be it that improvement must bury in its wake the myth of ancient heroes. We've exposed the extinction of .400 hitting as a sign of progress, not degradation—the paradoxical effect of declining variation as play improves and stabilizes, and as average contestants also approach the right wall of human limits.

Do not lament the loss of literally outstanding performance (largely a figment, in any case, of failings among the ordinary, not a mark of greater prowess among the best). Celebrate instead the immense improvement of average play. (I rather suspect that we would regard most operatic performances of 1850, and most baseball games of 1900, as sloppy and amateurish—not to mention the village squabbles that enter history as epic battles.) Do not lament our past ease in distinguishing the truly great. Celebrate instead the general excellence that makes professional sport so exciting today. And appreciate the need for subtlety and discernment that modern fans must develop to make proper assessments; we must all now be connoisseurs to appreciate our favorite games fully. Above all, remember that the possibility for transcendence never dies. We live for that moment, the truly unpredictable performance that shatters all expectations. We delight all the more in Dwight Gooden and Larry Bird because they stand out among a panoply of true stars. Besides, I really wrote this essay only because I have a hunch that I want to share (and we professor types need to set context before we go out on a limb): Wade Boggs is gonna hit .400 one of these years.

Horatio at the Bat, or Why Such a Lengthy Embryonic Period for The Serious Baseball Novel?

By MARK HARRIS

MANY PEOPLE EARNESTLY SAY that baseball novels are not about baseball; they are really about something else, some grander theme of life or death or God or theology, or they are really about art or morals, or they are mythical representations of America, legends, and therefore not about baseball, as they seem on the surface to be, or as they seem on the jacket to be—the jacket showing a man in what appears to be a baseball uniform sliding into a white cushion which appears to be a base on a baseball field.

This is to a very great extent what I want to get at—the idea that for a long time we haven't wanted to say that a novel about baseball is a novel about baseball because we wanted to believe it was about something else—something more respectable, something more serious, something, for example, a serious, studious, scholarly person could talk about without losing caste among his peers, without people thinking Oh Jones—Oh Malamud, Oh Roth—he's not really serious.

Baseball novels, baseball fiction, exists in the tradition of success literature, in which a deserving young man achieves his deserved success in life. And he was, of course, always that—he was deserving, he was young, he was a man—that is to say, he was a man but he was a boy with whom boys could identify even if their lives were remote from his, or his from theirs—he was American, pure in the sense that he had a name derived from England, he had blond hair or fiery red hair, he was spectacularly honest and clean-cut and fearless and heroic and he had a marvelous sense of humor. His parents were admirable and he loved them every minute. Baseball Joe calls his mother Momsey and his sister Sis.

Baseball Joe's last name is Matson, causing him to resemble, I once heard, Christy Mathewson of the New York Giants who, I have heard, was himself a reader of the books of Horatio Alger. Most readers know what I refer to when I speak of a book by Horatio Alger (there were dozens and dozens of books, but they were all one book). Some Alger titles: *Adrift in New York, Andy Grant's Pluck and Luck, Bound to Rise, Brave and Bold, Cash Boy, Do and Dare, Driven from Home, Erie Train Boy, Facing the World, Grit, Hector's Inheritance, Jed the Poor House Boy, Julius the Street Boy, Making His Way, Only an Irish Boy, Paul the Peddler, Phil the Fiddler, Risen from the Ranks, Shifting for Himself, Tom the Bootblack, Tony the Tramp, Try and Trust, Wait and Hope.* The basic book by Horatio Alger was a basic plan of the American dream, and it was also to a significant extent the basic plan of the novel about baseball.

In the Alger book *Mark Manning's Mission,* there is the hermit Anthony Mark. Mark's widowed mother. The hermit's nephew. The Squire and his bad son. The bad son's friend and crony. Well-plotted with interlocking characters, lots of incredible coincidences. You've read one you've read them all. You've also read Baseball Joe—at least *Baseball Joe in the Central League,* which I read after not having read any Baseball Joe for many years. This was the first and only Baseball Joe I picked up, as *Mark Manning's Mission* was the first and only Alger.

Summary of *Mark Manning's Mission: The Story of a Shoe Factory Boy*: Mark works for Squire Collins in the shoe factory. Mark hears the hermit Anthony groaning in his cabin and assists him. Lyman Taylor arrives to try to extort money from his uncle the hermit. (Lyman knows that the hermit has money, but Mark of course does not.) Tom and James accidentally shoot a cow through the eyes in the pasture and vow to blame it on Mark. Deacon Miller accuses Mark of having shot his cow and demands forty-five dollars. Mark's reply to Deacon Miller: "If I had shot your cow I wouldn't have run away, but I'd have gone right to you and told you about it, and I'd have paid you just as soon as I could."

Mark protests that the hermit is overpaying him for his services. Mark gives his money to his mother, a clean woman who is usually seen sewing. Lyman the rascal nephew realizes that Anthony likes Mark so much he is likely to leave him his fortune. Squire Collins is about to foreclose the house in which Mark's mother has been able to live at a most reasonable rent, but what the bad Squire does not know is that the hermit in his financial wisdom has bought out the Squire's business and thus made Mark the owner of the factory from which he was so recently discharged. Mark is now his recent boss's boss. "Mark," says the hermit, "is one whom I can train up for a responsible position. I am getting older every year, and when I am really old, I shall be glad to have a young man at my side upon whom I can shift the burden of my business. Do you think his mother would object?"

How does everybody come out? "James Collins is now a clerk in Newport, on a small salary, with which he is very much discontented, and from time to time asks a loan of his old schoolfellow Mark, to whom he is now compelled to look up. He has developed extravagant habits, and is always in debt. I greatly fear that neither his habits nor his fortunes will improve as he grows older. For our hero, Mark, and those who belong to him, we may anticipate brighter days and greater prosperity, as a fitting recompense of industry and good habits. THE END."

At the beginning of *Baseball Joe in the Central League* (by Lester Chadwick, 1914) Joe arrives home "swinging a heavy valise as though he enjoyed the weight of it. . . . 'Hello, mother,' he called gaily." (He loves his mother, as Mark Manning does.) He has come home from Yale to Riverside, a New England town. He'd rather be a professional baseball player. He can earn $1,500 a year, which is more than a minister makes. His mother wants him to be a minister. Father is an inventor. He has lost some money in investments. "'Oh, if that's all, we can soon fix that!' cried Joe, gaily. . . ." He has "infectious good-humor."

Although he is home only for a few days he has time to rescue a tramp (an outcast, like Alger's hermit) from death on the railroad tracks. Soon Joe himself is on a train going south. He has received a grand send-off from the home folks. Out of the window he sees "the same tramp he had saved from the freight train some days before." He overhears a man in another seat telling his traveling companion who that tramp is: "Old" Pop Dutton, formerly a great baseball player, now fallen among bad companions and drink. On this same trip a "modish young man" loses valuables from his "queer valise," and accuses Joe.

Lester Chadwick touches very briefly—in a dozen lines—on the theme which is to become basic to the baseball novel at the other end of Baseball Joe's century—the tension between individualism and teamwork. Baseball "was a fight for the survival of the fittest. . . . Understand me, I am not speaking against organized baseball. It is a grand thing, and one of the cleanest sports in the world. But what I am pointing out is that it is a business, and from a business standpoint everyone in it must do his best for himself. Each man, in a sense, is concerned only with his own success. Nor do I mean that this precludes a love of the club, and good teamwork. Far from it."

One Sunday Joe goes for a walk into the country. He hears the clatter of hoofs. Now you know he is going to make a rescue, in the tradition of the Alger hero. "A spirited horse, attached to a light carriage, dashed around a bend in the road, coming straight for Joe. And in the carriage was a young girl, whose fear-blanched face told that she realized her danger. A broken, dangling rein showed that she had tried in vain to stop the runaway. 'I've got to stop that horse!' gasped Joe." Luckily, "at his feet were several large and round, smooth stones. . . . 'If I could only hit him [the horse] on the head, and stun him so that he'd stop before he gets to the cliff!' thought Joe." He does so. After all, the large, round, smooth stones were the size of baseballs. Joe falls in love with the girl with the fear-blanched face, and she with him. Her name is Mabel, and the horse will recover. But a difficulty exists: Her brother is the fellow who accused Joe of stealing valuables from his queer valise. Can a nice girl, after all, love a thief? Joe will need to clear himself before this is over.

One day in an early game Joe does poorly, but he is consoled by an "old" man in the stands. It is the tramp whom Joe saved once and later saw from the train, the one-time great ballplayer. And not long afterward a telegram arrives from home: "Your father hurt in explosion. No danger of death, but may lose eyesight. If you can come home do so. Mother."

And there's another father-figure, Old Pop Dutton, not as old as I had thought—he seems to be under thirty—who becomes inspired through his association with Joe to get back into shape, forswear his bad habits, and return to baseball, which he does. But he, too, needs an operation, not an eye operation but an arm operation, and Joe has vowed that if Pittston wins the pennant, and Joe thereby wins extra money, he will pay for both operations in those days before Blue Cross.

Old Pop Dutton, repudiating his former low associates, finds out from a one-time underworld associate who stole the valuable objects from the queer valise belonging to Mabel's brother. Now Mabel knows that Joe is honest. The pennant race goes down to the last game. Joe is to pitch, but he is late to the park because that jealous teammate tampered with the regulator lever of his watch. Who did it? It was the faithless teammate Collin, the man who placed himself above team. Luckily, Joe is able to reach the park in the fifth inning and to help his team come from behind and win. "When the last batter had gone down to defeat in the first half of the ninth Joe drew off his glove and, oblivious to the plaudits of the crowd and his own mates, hurried to the dressing room." Everything works out. Everyone is exonerated who needed exoneration, and everyone's medical problems are solved—surgery for father, surgery for Pop.

Another book that carries the theme is *Highpockets*, by John R. Tunis. Highpockets is an outfielder for the Dodgers but he is not a team player. "Look here, Highpockets, why don't you quit thinking about your batting average and play for the team? Why don't you be a nice guy like the other boys on the club?" "Yessuh. I know a lotta nice guys don't win no ball games."

But Highpockets reforms. He is redeemed, saved, is no longer a loner on the ball club. "It was a different gang of ballplayers, and this was evident in many ways.... At last he was a part of the team, not just a long-ball hitter out there slugging for himself.... The fans there are also quick to recognize the right guy, the team player. So they yelled and yelled. At last Highpockets belonged to Brooklyn."

Regarding juvenile sports fiction, Michael Oriard in *Arete* (Fall, 1983), commented: "One of the things that makes the overwhelming majority of juveniles so deadeningly dull and similar is the lack of any distance between the hero and the ideal."

Highpockets was first published as late as 1948. There had still not been, as far as I know, a book about baseball which anyone could have thought of as art or as literature, except for Ring Lardner's *You Know Me Al*, published in 1914 and applauded by a number of people who took literature seriously. Among these were two very distinguished literary or learned people—H. L. Mencken and Virginia Woolf. Mencken relished the accuracy of Lardner's idiom, and Virginia Woolf saw the book as an authentic description of American society—that is, American life, for she uses the word "society" differently: Classless America, she said, was bound or unified by games, as England was bound by society.

Whatever the reason, *You Know Me Al* became famous in America, a landmark, perhaps, as Lardner's son John would contend in 1959, better known than read: "The impact of [its] original publication, forty-five years ago, was such that [its] fame has endured to a large extent by word of mouth, like that of New York's blizzard of 1888. . . . It's not necessary—as years of involuntary research have shown me—for someone to have read *You Know Me Al* to want to talk about it. I think that reading is better. . . ."

Ring Lardner wrote his own preface to a reprinting of the book, in March, 1925, one of your briefer prefaces—hardly a page—and the thing that is noteworthy about Lardner's preface is its implicit dismissal of the book as literature, Lardner's own refusal, at least, to take it seriously. He declines to challenge the idea of serious literature; he withdraws from any idea, therefore, that he himself might be a literary man.

PREFACE

The writer has been asked frequently, or perhaps not very often after all, two vital questions regarding the letters published in this book: (1) Are they actual letters or copies of actual letters? and (2) Who is the original of Jack Keefe?

The first question seemed highly complimentary until you thought it over and realized that no one with good sense could have asked it. Some of the letters run as long as a thousand words and there is only one person in the world who writes letters of that length. She is a sister-in-law of mine living in Indianapolis, and when she sits down to write a letter, she holds nothing back. But she is a Phi Beta and incapable of the mistakes in spelling and grammar that unfortunately have crept into this volume.

As for the other question, I have heretofore declined to reply to it, as a reply would have stopped the boys and girls from guessing, and their guesses have given me many a thrill. But now there are no ballplayers left whom they haven't guessed, from Noah to Bucky Harris, and I may as well give the correct answer. The original of Jack Keefe is not a ballplayer at all, but Jane Addams of Hull House, a former Follies girl.

An introduction to this book was written by Will Rogers, but the Scribner boys threw it out on the ground that it was better than the book. However, there was one remark of Mr. Rogers, which I think should be preserved. Referring to me, he wrote: "He is undoubtedly the biggest—" The rest of the sentence is so blurred as to be indecipherable.

The writer wishes to acknowledge his indebtedness to Mayo brothers, Ringling brothers, Smith brothers, Rath brothers, the Dolly sisters, and former President Buchanan for their aid in instructing him in the technical terms of baseball, such as "bat," "ball," "pitcher," "foul," "sleeping car," and "sore arm."

R. W. L.
March, 1925.

The tale, or at least the series of letters from Keefe, begins with a letter from Jack Keefe to his friend Al, whom we never meet, from Terre Haute September 6, telling him he (Jack) has been sold from the Central League to the White Sox. In December Jack goes to Chicago to meet for contract discussion with Mr. Comiskey, owner of the White Sox. He waits two days to meet Mr. Comiskey, and reports the meeting on December 16, in the following letter:

> Dear Friend Al: Well I will be home in a couple of days now but I wanted to write you and let you know how I come out with Comiskey. I signed my contract yesterday afternoon. He is a great old fellow Al and no wonder everybody likes him. He says Young man will you have a drink? But I was to smart and wouldn't take anything. He says You was with Terre Haute? I says Yes I was. He says Doyle tells me you were pretty wild. I says Oh no I got good control. He says Well do you want to sign? I says Yes if I get my figure. He asks What is my figure and I says three thousand dollars per annum. He says Don't you want the office furniture too? Then he says I thought you was a young ballplayer and I didn't know you wanted to buy my park.
>
> We kidded each other back and forth like that a while and then he says You better go out and get the air and come back when you feel better. I says I feel O.K. now and I want to sign a contract because I have got to get back to Bedford. Then he calls the secretary and tells him to make out my contract. He give it to me and it calls for two hundred and fifty a month. He says You know we always have a city serious here in the fall where a fellow picks up a good bunch of money. I hadn't thought of that so I signed up. My yearly salary will be

> fifteen hundred dollars besides what the city serious brings me. And that is only for the first year. I will demand three thousand or four thousand dollars next year.
>
> I would of started home on the evening train but I ordered a suit of clothes from a tailor over on Cottage Grove and it won't be done till to-morrow. It's going to cost me twenty bucks but it ought to last a long time. Regards to Frank and the bunch.
>
> Your Pal, Jack.

Lardner apparently never thought of *You Know Me Al* or any of his other work as literature. He wrote for a living as a newspaper writer and magazine writer, for enormous fees to support expensive habits. As the world viewed him, so he viewed himself: a writer who wrote about baseball as a sports writer, not a literary person, even if he wrote stories, and even if one of his stories grew to the length of a book.

You Know Me Al emerged from no baseball tradition of baseball writing, but it did emerge from the tradition of the American vernacular. The best-known novel in that tradition is undoubtedly *Huckleberry Finn*, and one of the best-known novels in that tradition in our own time is *The Catcher in the Rye*, whose narrator, Holden Caulfield, tells us that his favorite writer (apart from his brother D. B.) is Ring Lardner.

The tradition *You Know Me Al* clearly rejects, however, is the tradition of the Horatio Alger story. Jack Keefe does not make good in any sense Alger would approve. He has not troubled himself to speak well, to become literate. He spells by ear. When he threatens to jump to the Federal League he reveals that he has never developed corporate loyalties. His marital difficulties are mean and violent. No Momsey, no Sis. He thinks about money on every page. He drinks, he carouses, he tells jokes about underwear.

Even so, we like him, or at least I certainly liked him when I read him as a boy in the decade of the thirties in Mount Vernon, New

York, and must have read Lardner's shorter stories in *The Saturday Evening Post*, especially if they were baseball stories, since I sold the *Post* from door to door. He was never mere hearsay for me, as he was for so many of the people John Lardner encountered.

The Southpaw appeared in 1953. When, a mere 34 years later, Dr. Vartan Gregorian invited me to talk about sports and American culture he also invited me to feel free to discuss, among other baseball books, my own. I thought I would do so if in the process of exploring the subject my own work appeared relevant. I wouldn't want to drag myself in. Then I discovered something in the writings of Peter C. Bjarkman: I had never thought about it in this way, although my wife had mentioned it to me several times over the years, and now I see how true it is. Bjarkman writes: "Baseball fiction is itself certainly not an exclusive phenomenon of the second half of the twentieth century. An established tradition of boys' novels and pulp fiction produced enough volumes on the national game to fill over forty pages of entries in Anton Grobani's first extensive bibliography of baseball literature.... Yet the first serious adult baseball fiction (if one excludes perhaps Ring Lardner's dozen best stories and one major novel), did not appear until the early 1950's, with Bernard Malamud's *The Natural* and Mark Harris's Henry Wiggen trilogy. This was more than a full century after baseball had been crowned the American national game. Why, then, such a lengthy embryonic period for the serious baseball novel?"

But if *The Southpaw* was in some ways the first of the realistic tradition of the baseball novel it also belonged to the end of the tradition of the sentimental Alger-like baseball novel: my boy Henry *does* succeed, *does* grow rich, even as he mocks the Alger tradition. That's a paradox I was left to settle elsewhere in my work, if I could.

When the time of my life arrived to look behind me and identify my sources I behaved as if I had not cared for Lardner at all. I tended to discount him as an influence, even as I tended to discount the influence upon me of the Baseball Joe books—right there on the jacket of the first edition of *The Southpaw*, the words of the anonymous publisher's publicist: "Obviously Henry has nothing in common with the sentimental, saccharine and completely improbable sagas which keep bobbing up under the general category of 'baseball books.'"

But of course my book did have a great deal in common with that old sentimental category, and what it had in common was the Horatio Alger tradition from which I emerged as a boy-reader and perpetuated as a young-man writer.

In 1952, just a few months before *The Southpaw* was published, Bernard Malamud appeared with a novel called *The Natural*, which angered me in the way I had always been angered by ignorance about baseball.

Malamud just wasn't realistic baseball. For example, he gave his players "cleats" to wear, but baseball players wear "spikes." I reviewed the book in my angry tone for the Minneapolis newspaper. I lived then in Minneapolis, when its baseball team—the Millers—played outdoors, not indoors, and nobody dreamed that in 1987, the Millers, alias Twins, would win a World Series indoors wearing cleats.

But if I thought my whole approach to my writing about baseball was different from Malamud's I was mistaken. One thing we deeply shared was our self-consciousness about what we were doing: We were insisting we were creating literature just as earnestly as Ring Lardner, forty years earlier, had insisted that he was NOT creating literature. I was at the time of the publication of *The Southpaw* a graduate student at the University of Minnesota, and I certainly did not want my professors to think of me as frivolous. Therefore, I claimed a literary standing for my work which was above the old-time Baseball Joe sentimentality. If anybody wanted to know where my inspiration came from it came from *Huckleberry Finn*—so widely respected in the English Department—not from Baseball Joe or even from Ring Lardner.

Malamud too was trying to make his way in academic life. "During my first year at Oregon State," he has written, "I wrote *The Natural*, begun before leaving New York City. Baseball had interested me, especially its comic aspects, but I wasn't able to write about the game until I transformed game into myth, via Jessie Weston's Percival legend with an assist by T. S. Eliot's 'The Waste Land' plus the lives of several ballplayers I had read, in particular Babe Ruth's and Bobby Feller's. The myth enriched the baseball lore as feats of magic transformed the game."

So you see, for Malamud's professors, his employers, baseball had to be comic, a myth. It could not be simply (and this was my problem, too, at the time) part of the writer's fund of memory, a playing out of sandlot pleasure: It had to be serious and bookish. It couldn't be just baseball. It had to be mythic, symbolic, or it had to offer—this was the course of my own thinking about my book—a self-conscious dissociation of its author from the low-brow tradition of Horatio Alger and Baseball Joe.

From *Arete* Fall 1984, re: *The Natural*: "Many a glassy-eyed scholar has ravaged *The Golden Bough* searching for one more applicable motif to attach to [*The Natural*]. It has been . . . compared to every mythical personage from Apollonius of Rhodes to Shoeless Joe Jackson. Pausing only occasionally for breath, these professional potentates bombarded the halls and towers of academe with their oracular declarations and their sacerdotal pronouncements. Memo is Delilah, she is Calypso, she is Circe. Iris is Demeter, Isis, Gea, etcetera, ad infinitum, summa cum laude."

All this is capsulized very well by a scholar named Ben Siegel in his reflections about Philip Roth's *The Great American Novel* (1973). Siegel in *Contemporary Literature* in 1975: Roth in recent years has moved "increasingly in his fiction from the realistic to the outlandish and fantastic. . . . Asked why he chose baseball Roth replied, 'Because whaling has already been used.'" Baseball, says Siegel, "enables Roth not only to belabor the self-inflating legends of macho and camaraderie upon which several sports-loving generations have been raised, but to expose the Boys of Summer for the dirty old men and dirty young men many of them have been all the time. Roth long delayed writing a baseball novel. Despite his fondness for the game . . . he had to overcome, he confesses, his own 'perversity . . . contrariness . . . snobbishness,' had to convince himself the sport offered the 'seriousness or profundity' he believed a novel subject should have. Two factors, he claims, changed his mind. The first was that he finally gained, at this late point in his career, a needed 'confidence' in his own 'literary impulses.' He needed that confidence to renew his 'pursuit of the unserious'. . . ."

So Philip Roth was coming out of the closet—the heterosexual closet—in the late 1960s in *Portnoy's Complaint.* Masturbation wasn't naughty enough for Philip—now baseball.

Not only Roth, but scores—hundreds—of scholars, were liberated at last to read and write about baseball. The most hospitable place for sports scholarship is the journal *Arete,* whose editors and contributors usually have backgrounds in fields distant from sports literature. I hear of annual meetings and regional meetings of the Sport Literature Association related to *Arete,* complete with a varied program, a keynote speaker, hotel data, car rental information, and all the characteristics of the Modern Language Association. When these assembled scholars go off after their sessions to a sporting event—football, baseball, whatever—they go with that ideal clean feeling of one who, even in his recreational hours, is tending to serious business, like a wine-taster. Notice the modest industry in baseball scholarship.

My own favorite scholar is Peter C. Bjarkman of Lafayette, Indiana, upon whom I have gratefully depended for background information. One interesting item of Bjarkman's extensive work is his notice of another: Professor Myron J. Smith's *Baseball: A Comprehensive Bibliography* "with nearly 22,000 entries," says Bjarkman, "has advanced baseball scholarship to the realm of serious status within the social sciences."

One of Bjarkman's comprehensive documents is "an overview," as he calls it, of serious adult baseball fiction since 1973. I can no longer count baseball novels on my fingers. Bjarkman counts eighty baseball novels during the past two decades, and for every novel multiple reviews and articles, soon to be followed by academic dissertations. For example: *Baseball: The Origin and Development of the Game to 1903; The Linguistic Accommodation of a Cultural Innovation as Illustrated by the Game of Baseball in the Spanish Language of Puerto Rico; American Cultural Values as Reflected in the Architectural Evolution and Criticism of the Modern Baseball Stadium.*

What are some of the "serious" baseball novels? They include at least two novels by women and at least two novels—not the same two—featuring the first woman to enter the big leagues as a player, a theme which also appears in several books written as children's or juvenile literature.

I've read some of these authors and the most striking thing about them, to begin with, is their diversity. In the novels of baseball during the past twenty years the tradition of Horatio Alger has been replaced by the focus of fantasy sometimes, realism sometimes, problem solving, ventures into myth, symbolism, baseball futurism, baseball science-fiction, into the very homosexuality for which Horatio Alger was condemned and fired from his ministry only 125 years earlier, drugs and other illegal or shadowy activities which make the alleged thievery of Baseball Joe sound tame indeed.

For example, a story by Ray Blount, Jr., in *Sudden Fiction*—four pages called "Five Ives." The player calls home to tell his brother about his first game in the big leagues. Spanish-speaking guys and black guys in the locker room. The manager is eating what looks like a sandwich of Franco-American spaghetti. "I'm dressing next to Hub Kopf. Yeah, right, used to have the crippled children commercial. He is talking to Junior Wren. And here's what they're saying. "Your *niece*! How could you...." "Axly it was more my half niece." "How the hell?" "Anyway, she was adopted, I think." "You *think*. You didn't *know*." "Anyway, she was in these little shorts and halter, and she had this raspberry wine . . . and I gave her a little bump. Next morning I felt so bad I quit smoking." The next thing he knows someone has pressed a pill on him. "Five milligrams!" He pinch-hits with orders to bunt. He twice fails. So he hits a home run instead. And that's the secret of *his* success, such as it is, a long way from the virtues announced by Horatio Alger.

Joseph Maiolo's story in *Ploughshares*, Vol. 13, Nos. 2 & 3, "Covering Home," is an example of the modern story in which we do not even find out how the crucial game turns out. Perhaps this is stressing the uncertainty of the future, unlike the Alger story or

Baseball Joe. It begins: "Coach discovered Danny's arm when Danny's parents were splitting up," and when Danny pitches: "Each time he throws he imagines the big mitt to be the face of somebody he hates. But he doesn't dislike enough people that he can change with each pitch, so he uses movie and TV criminals and assorted villains from board games and videos. He has taught himself to do it over and over, using Pye's mitt like a face in a hole in the wall at a carnival. Works pretty well, too. They're in the playoffs."

Whatever happened to Baseball Joe? He's gone. Where? I think he has been converted to the baseball biography, and followed the course of the novel out of the tradition of sentimentality into the tradition of realism.

Little League: An Idea Whose Time Has Come ... And Gone

By JAY FELDMAN

MY WIFE AND I were watching our nine-year-old son's Little League game when she turned to me and said, "There's something missing here, but I'm not sure what it is." I knew what she meant, but I couldn't put my finger on it either.

That weekend, my son accompanied me to my over-30s baseball team's practice. There were a few other kids there, and we gave them a bat and ball and sent them to the other end of the park. Very soon, the exuberant sounds from their game caught my ear; I looked over, and at the sight of them leaping and frisking unselfconsciously about, I knew at once what had been missing from that Little League game: joy—the spontaneous, unrestrained exhilaration of kids having fun.

Why don't kids seem to be having fun in Little League? The deterrent, I believe, is the adults—and not just the overly aggressive, winning-is-everything types who are living out their unfulfilled sports dreams through their children. The problem is the whole pervasive adult structure that dominates the Little League program.

To begin with, the volunteer system upon which Little League is based is no longer effective. In the late 1930s, when Little League was first instituted, adults with real baseball knowledge and experience were drawn to the coaching ranks. Today, because Little League has grown so large (7,000 leagues and 2.5 million youngsters worldwide), any adult with good intentions can be a coach, so you often have people in charge who know little about the game.

Case in point: last season, my son showed up at practice with a wooden bat, but the coaches told him it was prohibited. Imagine, disallowing a wooden bat? A couple of weeks later, though, during a game, my son noticed a player on the opposing team using one. He told his coach, who pointed it out to the umpire. "So what?" was the arbiter's response. "There's nothing in the rules against wooden bats." Now, how can I tell my kid to listen to his coaches if they don't even know the rules?

Little League has become a glorified baby-sitting service. The players not on the field are expected to sit on the bench and "behave" themselves. This not only goes against the nature of young children, who need to be running around and blowing off steam; it goes against the grain of the game. Baseball is not a genteel activity where you "behave" yourself; it's an intense competition where you let it all hang out, and if your actions are inappropriate or offensive, you suffer the consequences.

Little League is too darned organized. T-ball, preminors, minors, majors—for pity's sake, give the kids some room to breathe. They're started way too young, at six years old, when most kids don't have the attention span necessary to carry out an activity that takes more than a few minutes. Watch them in the field; they're turning circles, chewing their gloves, picking their noses—everything but concentrating on the ball game. You have to ask yourself, "Do these kids really want to be here?"

When I was a kid, we organized our games ourselves. You grabbed your glove, bat and ball (if you had those things), headed down to the park or schoolyard, and found a game—anywhere from two on a side to full teams. Nobody had to tell us what to do. We played many variations of baseball—the kind of game depended on the number of kids, type of playing field, equipment available, and so on—and if the situation called for it, we'd invent the rules to fit what we had.

You don't see that today. When a San Francisco friend of mine told his eleven-year old to go out and find a ball game one day, the boy said, "Kids don't do that anymore, Dad. We only play if it's scheduled."

Not only are the kids not organizing their own games, which brings with it the feeling of belonging; they're also not using their imaginations to create the rules that are needed for improvised play. Moreover—and this is truly unfortunate—they aren't getting the chance to resolve the conflicts that arise in the course of competition because the adults arbitrate everything for them. The ball field should be a place for kids to learn the skills necessary for settling differences. Instead, they sit by while the adults go at it, often displaying behavior that would be admonished were it manifested by the kids.

Case in point: not long ago, I saw my son's game delayed fifteen minutes while the coaches and the umpire hotly argued a situation. The parents on the sidelines shouted rude remarks. Finally, one kid yelled, "Hey, you guys, quit wasting our time!" Poor sportsmanship all around.

We would never have let an argument go on that long when we were kids. If a conflict was not resolvable in a reasonable amount of time, we invoked the ubiquitous "do-over." Even in a case where one side was clearly right but the other wouldn't give in, someone yelled, "Do-over," i.e., repeat the play, and the game went on. The injured party compromised for the sake of keeping the game going. We were learning popular democracy, practicing to be citizens.

Due to the constant adult presence in Little League, the kids don't have to take any initiative. The adults do it all. The parents pay the money, and the child gets a uniform. When we wanted uniforms, we had to figure out a way to raise the money, and when we got it together, we went to the sporting goods store and ordered the uniforms ourselves. It was a big deal for us, and those uniforms were *ours*.

Today the kids own none of it. No wonder there's no joy. All ideas and institutions have their time and place. In 1939 Little League was a fresh concept; fifty years later it's become an archaic ritual that has lost its original vitality. We're beating a dead horse; we'd do better to just give it a decent burial. Do-over. Give the game back to the kids; if they want to play baseball, they'll work it out for themselves.

The Minoans—A Whole New Ball Game

By JOHN S. BOWMAN

ALEXANDER GRAHAM BELL, it is alleged, once remarked that if he had known more about electricity, he would never have invented the telephone. And indeed, one of the pleasures, if not profits, of the freelancer's trade is occasionally to make some new connection—to discover links or patterns that those working in more defined disciplines simply have overlooked. Call it "lateral thinking" or serendipity or just the random insights of a dilettante, but once in a while the non-expert, the non-specialist, sees things that those who know so much have failed to see.

An appropriate example is the case of Michael Ventris. Although an architect by profession, Ventris possessed an intense amateur's interest in solving linguistic problems. In pursuing this passion, Ventris—not the great philologists or archaeologists or academic scholars—finally solved the mystery of Linear B, the script used in the Minoan-Mycenaean world between about 1500 BC and 1250 BC. Ever since 1900, when Arthur Evans turned up the first of the tablets inscribed with what he called Linear B, it had been a standing challenge to the experts to decipher the language being recorded. In 1952 Ventris, freed from the various preconceptions and prejudices of the many experts who had been working on the problem, established that the language recorded was simply early Greek.

Without claiming to have scaled a similar "Everest"—as Ventris' achievement was characterized at the time—nor in any way presuming to compare myself to Ventris, I am here as a fellow amateur to announce that I believe I have solved another of the vexatious puzzles of Minoan inscriptions. Beyond that, my solution involves two of the primary "texts" of America's past whose anniversaries were observed in 1988 but whose true significance, it now turns out, was never dreamed of. And finally, I am here to claim that my discovery also bears on a debate that continues to disturb students of the archaeology of American life: If Abner Doubleday didn't, then just who did invent the game of baseball? How these otherwise remote worlds have come to be linked confirms my opening point—that perhaps only a non-academic like myself, at present engaged in "working" various fields, would be free to make such a perception.

My association with the Minoans goes back more than 30 years to my first visit to Crete; ensuing years of visiting, reading, thinking, and writing about the many aspects of Minoan civilization have made me not a scholar but a well-informed student of things Minoan. My association with baseball does not go that far back—in matters of its history, that is. Like most American boys, I grew up playing baseball and following my favorite teams and players, but it has been only in the last few years that I have become involved in researching the history of the game. And one of the ongoing issues remains—who "invented" baseball? As all half-knowledgeable students have long accepted, Abner Doubleday of Cooperstown, New York, did not. But this has left open the question of just what the game's origins are.

Histories of the sport traditionally cite some references to similar games in English books of the 18th century, then vaguely refer to medieval bat-and-ball games. (For some reason, a ball game played at Easter time near the Cathedral of Rheims is always dragged in.) Then there are the obligatory references to fertility rites among the ancients, with perhaps some dubious reproduction of an Egyptian wall-painting. But none of this really pins down the origins of the game of baseball as Americans know it. The question abides.

One side of the Phaestos Disc. The pictographs, or hieroglyphics, have been drawn as carefully as possible from the actual disc by an expert (not the author, so he cannot be charged with weighting the evidence). Each "field" has been numbered for convenient reference. Most authorities have long agreed that the inscription begins at this field numbered 1 and spirals into the center.

So it was that I—sensitized to the question of the origins of baseball and with my deep-seated awareness of Minoan issues—came to stumble on "the figure in the carpet." It started with an article that I was sent by yet another person claiming to have solved one of the major mysteries of the Minoan world: the inscription on the Phaestos Disc. This baked clay disc—some six and three-quarter inches in diameter and about a half inch thick—takes its name from Phaestos, the second (after Knossos) of the great Minoan palaces excavated on Crete early in this century. But where Evans excavated Knossos in the full glare of the public record of that time, the Italians who excavated Phaestos continued to work all but ignored (a matter we shall have reason to reconsider later). Eventually there would be a small room at one side of the Palace of Phaestos designated as the site where the disc was found; because of this context, the disc was dated to about 1650-1600 BC; since nothing like it has turned up in any other Minoan site, some scholars have decided that the disc was imported into Crete. (Lycia, along the coast of present-day Turkey, is the current favorite as a point of provenance). What is known is that eventually the disc was turned over to the Cretan-Greek archaeological authorities and that it has ended up as one of the prominent displays in the Archaeological Museum in Iraklion.

But if the disc's exact provenance is somewhat mysterious, the inscription on its sides is even more troublesome. For the Phaestos Disc is imprinted on both sides with a total of 242 signs; this total, however, is made up of only 45 *different* signs; these are arranged in 30 boxes, or fields, on one side, 31 on the other, each box separated by vertical lines. What makes it most distinct, indeed unique in the ancient world, is that each sign was impressed into the wet clay by a metal stamp, one for each of the 45 signs—in effect, the first example of "movable type."

Should anyone suspect that I am loading up my own case, here is what Sterling Dow and John Chadwick, two unimpeachable authorities, have to say in the *Cambridge Ancient History*:

> All the indications show that the two sides of the Disc were both the work of one man, at one time. For each different sign he had one stamp; he used each stamp over and over, as often as the text demanded. On each side he ran the text in a spiral. Evidently he began, as is natural, (the evidence is virtually compelling although disagreement persists) at the circumference, and wound into the center. To guide the reader's eye, a continuous line was incised, tracing the course of the spiral. On

> each side the beginning is marked; the other end, at the center, is also unmistakable.
>
> The signs are blocked off in groups, each group delimited by a vertical line joined at the other end to the spiral line. Thus each group is in its own box.

As these two scholars recognize, there is disagreement over such details as whether the inscription should be read from edge to center, or center to edge, clockwise or counter-clockwise, etc. But the real problem lies in the signs themselves and what language they are recording. The signs are usually referred to as pictographs, but whether they are ideograms (signs referring to an idea or concept) or a syllabary (each sign sounded to form a syllable) or functioning in some other way, still has to be decided. Even leaving that in abeyance for now, the question arises as to what kind of text is being recorded. Attempts and solutions have been offered from the time the disc was first published, and because there are repetitions of the various signs and groupings—obviously, with only 45 signs to make up the total of 242 in 61 boxes—the tendency has been to read it as a poem or song—what Evans called a "chaunt."

This does not seem at all far-fetched: clearly it is a special object—nothing like it has been found in any other Minoan site—and it seems reasonable to assume that it was a highly significant text. Numerous attempts have been made to decipher it, concluding usually that it is a hymn or prayer or fertility rite or an astronomical chart or a ritual-ceremonial text or whatever. And numerous claims have also been made as to which language has been recorded: Hittite, Semitic, Egyptian, and virtually every other ancient language has been named. But most reputable scholars have rejected them all (including Greek). Every time someone has come forth crying *Eureka!*, other experts have managed to throw cold water on it.

The latest of these attempts that I am aware of is the aforementioned article sent to me; it is by H. Peter Aleff, and appeared in an Indian newspaper, *Mandakini.* The author argues that the Phaestos Disc should be seen in the line of board games that are accepted as being part of the oldest civilizations, particularly the type known as "race games" in which the game simulates or re-enacts the "race" of the heavenly bodies—the celestial cycles that played a role in so many aspects of ancient people's lives. In this interpretation of the Phaestos Disc, the signs and their boxes are not recording a text but are symbolic fields representing phases of the sun. But as this interpretation proceeds, it becomes an increasingly ingenious and murky one—layered with mythology, etymology, cosmology, and several other "ologies" until it is no longer so clear just what is involved.

What matters here, though, is that this article happened to come across my desk at the very time I was looking into a particular area of baseball history—namely, baseball as it has been taken over into American popular culture: songs, poetry, and such. And perhaps it was because this subject was on my mind—being sung subliminally, so to speak—that I happened to have a sudden *apercu* while I was trying to make sense of this interpretation of the Phaestos Disc. As I looked closely at the pictographs on one side of the disc, I was struck by a curious resemblance between some of them and certain familiar objects: a ball ... a bat ... a round structure ... running men ... a female figure .... Then I noticed what all decipherers of the disc have remarked on: the signs were repeated, if not in an immediately recognizable rhythmical pattern, at least with enough of one to suggest a refrain. Hhhhmmmm ... a song . . . the recurrent balls and bats and round structures ....

At first I was merely toying with the notion, but suppose, I said to myself, just suppose I were to assign the word "ball" to one sign, the word "stadium" or "park" to another, the word "action" or "game" to the running man, "strike" to the unusual looking bat. Ah, but then what was that sign for the female doing in the midst of all this? But then I vaguely recalled that the all-but-forgotten verse to the song—now forcing itself onto my lips—involved a young woman—indeed as I recalled, the words of the chorus were ones she was addressing to her beau.

At that moment I did not have the verse, but I realized that the chorus would, in any case, come at the end of the text. Why not work backwards, then—assigning the known words of the chorus to the final boxes, spiraling backwards from the center of the disc? And as I did so, everything began to fall into place: "ball," "park," signs I now realized could stand for "one," "two," "three," my sign for "strike"—they all seemed to fit! The real clincher, however, came when I was able to identify a small oval object as a nut and another peculiar pictograph—all scrunched up—it was popcorn!

By now most of those reading this have undoubtedly jumped to a conclusion. I was determined to proceed with more caution. I confess, though, to high excitement as I rushed off to a nearby university's library, ransacked all the songbooks, and finally came up with one that included the sought-for verse as well as the chorus. I photocopied it, rushed home, and flung myself down to my worksheets with the disc. And my god—they fit! With the remaining pictographs, I was now able to start at the first box and assign the words of the verse to the signs. One by one, they fell into place. Not always on a simple one-on-one basis, it must be admitted—not a straightforward pictograph for each word or phrase. Because it had already been apparent that this script was like Egyptian hieroglyphs in that its signs functioned in several ways: Some represented the actual object (as a ball or bat); some represented an idea or concept (a fuzzy bat representing a strike, a running man signalled the activity, the game); others seemed to be used simply for their sounds, as in a syllabary or alphabet. But allowing for some discrepancies, some repositionings of phrases or words (to make a rhyme, perhaps), and a couple of inevitably inexplicable points, I had to conclude that this inscription on the Phaestos Disc was essentially the words to "Take Me Out to the Ball Game." The song was published in 1908, but at that moment this date did not seem to be of any consequence.

I don't mind admitting that as I leaned back from my desk, I felt much as Ventris must have felt when he first saw the crucial tripod confirming his decipherment, or as Champollion felt when he realized he could read the royal cartouche. Could this be—the Minoans had a song that effectively anticipated "Take Me Out to the Ball Game"?

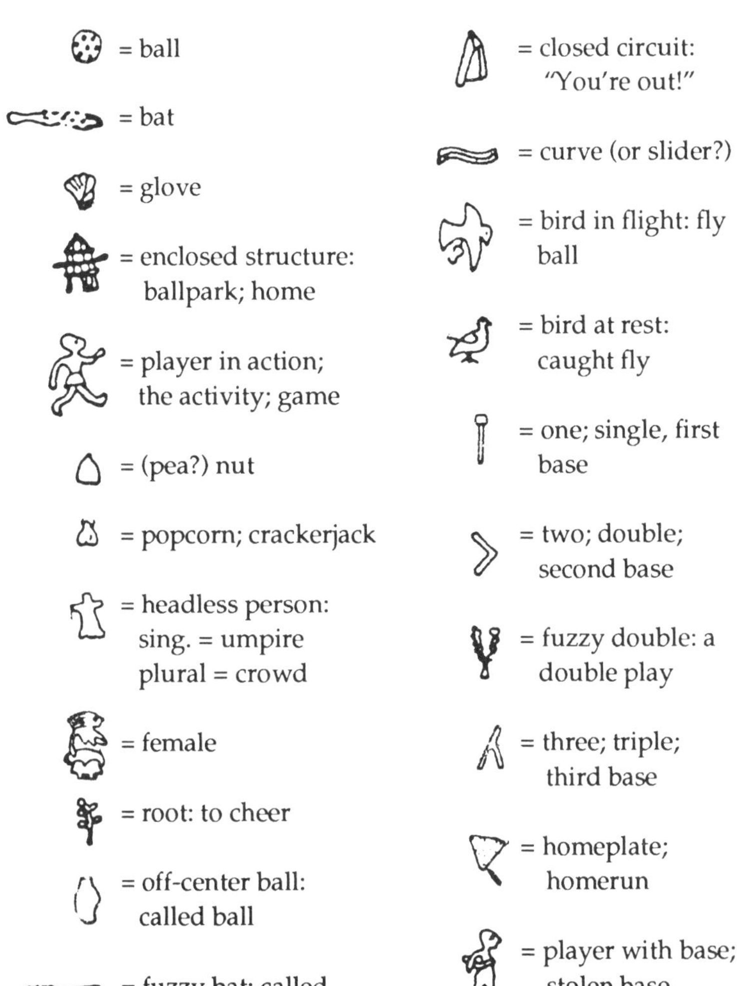

The author's first efforts at deciphering the signs on the Phaestos Disc led to the discovery of this basic vocabulary. The sheer number of baseball-related words and phrases suggest that baseball was quite popular in Minoan times.

: nut (!!) + two + three + ? + out: "One, two, three strikes, you're out!"

: glove + nut + popcorn (crackerjack) + double play *and* a double (= cancelled out: it doesn't matter): "(Buy me) some peanuts and crackerjack, I don't care (if I never get back)."

: root + home + ballpark: "So, it's root, root, root for the home team."

Some translations of boxes from the first side of the Phaestos Disc, using the vocabulary deciphered by the author.

True, much has been made of the Minoans as lovers of sport—but bull-leaping was a far cry from baseball. Homer, writing of the Mycenaean world that overlapped the end of the Minoans', briefly described some ball-based game but there was nothing suggesting anything approaching the game we know as baseball. But here was irrefutable evidence of baseball being played as early as 1600 BC—complete with "peanuts and crackerjacks!"

After I calmed down slightly, I began to deal with the question of just how this text could possibly have turned up as the words to a song attributed to one Jack Norworth. Just for something tangible to hang on to, I reached over for my copy of a guide to the Archaeological Museum of Iraklion to see if it might offer any hints as to the history of the Phaestos Disc—and suddenly, it jumped off the page: The disc had turned up in 1908! The very year that "Take Me Out to the Ball Game" was published.

Then something else clicked into place: It has always been said that one of the unusual things about the songwriter, Jack Norworth, and the composer of the melody, Albert von Tilzer, is that neither had ever been to a baseball game. This seems to have been publicized from the moment the song appeared, yet it is not something that most authors would have boasted about. But what if it is seen as an admission that the author had to make—to avoid being exposed to unwanted publicity. Both Norworth and von Tilzer were well-known Tin Pan Alley types early in this century; their friends would have known their habits; in order to put the matter to rest from the outset, they had to admit they had never attended a ballgame. Yet we are asked to believe that they composed this archetypal song of baseball!

At that stage in my speculations, I was willing to settle on the idea that the Minoans were much "in the air" at that time. The great Minoan palaces were being unearthed—Phaestos simultaneously with Knossos, as a matter of fact, although as mentioned earlier the Italians worked away at Phaestos in obscurity while each of Evans' finds was reported breathlessly in the media of the day. So my working hypothesis went this way: Norworth and von Tilzer were sophisticated Broadwayites, well known for their popular and catchy songs; someone associated with the Phaestos excavations had translated the text and then approached at least Norworth (we may never know if Von Tilzer was aware of the antiquity of the words he set so appropriately to music: At this point, little is known about Minoan music—perhaps later research will be able to establish the actual tune of the text on the Phaestos Disc). And then, according to my theory, once the Disc was turned over to the Archaeological Museum in 1908, Norworth and von Tilzer were free to bring out their version. Who would ever connect this dark disc in a remote archaeological museum with the bright lights of Broadway?

That still left me confronting a gap in time between the discovery of the Phaestos Disc and its public appearance in 1908, both in the Iraklion Museum and on Tin Pan Alley. Just on the most literal level of transportation in those days, there had to be some fairly generous period allowed. But then I remembered: The Italians, along with Cretans and Greeks, had been rummaging around ancient sites on Crete for many years before the well-publicized excavations of Evans (a fact not generally known to this day, for the myth of Evans as lone progenitor of the Minoan civilization dies hard). In particular, I recalled, the pioneering work had been done by the archaeologist

Federigo Helbherr (Italian, despite that surname), who from the early 1880s was turning up finds in the south-central region of Crete where Phaestos is located. Halbherr's most sensational find, at least until now, has been the Law Code of Gortyna, a Dorian Greek code dated to about 500 BC. (Most of it seems to pertain to civil laws, such as inheritance and adoption, but in retrospect there are provisions that sound suspiciously like the "reserve clause" that so long dominated organized baseball—that code might well repay a second reading.)

It is dangerous to make an accusation against a person of Halbherr's reputation, especially since he cannot defend himself, but the fact is that there has always been some question as to the exact finding of the Phaestos Disc. The literature is laced with the suspicions of the archaeological community, but quoting one reference—the already cited *Cambridge Ancient History* source, by Dow and Chadwick—should suffice: "An instance not merely of writing but an approximation to printing, immense in potentiality but null in effect—a freak—came to light in 1908, when L. Pernier stated that he discovered in the Palace of Phaestos a round clay disc covered on both sides with stamped signs." For now we may leave that interjected "freak" aside, but the fact remains that the phrasing "Pernier stated that he discovered" is not the way archaeologists speak of an accepted truth.

Yes, the exact provenance of the Phaestos Disc has always been problematic. And what I began to realize is that it might well have been found some time before 1908 and then spirited off the island by someone hoping to make a neat profit. After all, that is exactly what happened with the renowned Snake Goddess in the Boston Museum of Fine Arts. Evans, despite the closely observed excavation he conducted at Knossos, was unable to prevent someone from "kidnapping" this statuette; exactly when or how or by whom is not known, but somehow it ended up in the Boston Museum. If this could happen to such an obviously valuable work as the Snake Goddess, I find it most plausible to accept that someone was able to get off of Crete with a rather drab clay disc.

Then, once the disc arrived in a metropolitan center such as

Paris or London, it would have been offered in total secrecy. And gradually two possibilities would have presented themselves. Those who simply collected objects for their aesthetic attractions would hardly have cared about this little black disc. Meanwhile, an expert knowledgeable enough to figure out what the inscription revealed would also have realized that to publish this finding would ruin him in the eyes of fellow scholars. Imagine claiming that the text on an ancient Cretan disc described a baseball game! No, both connoisseur of art and scholarly expert would have refused to be associated with the disc. And so it was returned to Crete, where it "surfaced" in 1908.

To be sure, such an explanation left me with a "missing link:" There had to be some individual who could move between these two worlds—Cretan archaeology and American popular song. Someone who could bridge a Minoan inscription and a show business lyric. I was prepared to accept that such a person must have existed, even if I could never identify him, and obviously he, or an intermediary, had passed the translation on to Jack Norworth. The result was "Take Me Out to the Ball Game."

Astounding, is it not? Enough to make any freelancer's fame and fantasy. Indeed, in the first few days after my discovery, I was content to walk around my house and simply contemplate how I would best release this news to the world at large. I told no one but my wife in those first few days—it was like holding the winning ticket to a million-dollar lottery. But then one night, in the very middle of the night, I suddenly awoke: Wait a minute, I said to myself—for by then I was wide awake—I may have deciphered one side of the disc, but I had completely overlooked a disconcerting fact: There are *two* sides—and the second one also has an inscription. How to explain that away, Mr. Freelance Genius?

I was so unsettled by this realization that I could not even bear to get up and look at the inscription on the second side of the disc. The next morning, though, I forced myself to do so. Of course I had seen this second side often enough not to be surprised that it bore considerable resemblance to the first side—the one I had now translated. Although a few signs were missing and some new ones were added, many of the by-now familiar signs jumped out at me: the ball, the park, the "one," "two," "three," the game in action, the strike. . . . Clearly this second side had something to do with the first. But in some ways, instead of strengthening my case, this realization seemed to weaken it: If there was another ancient Minoan text using so many of the same words, and there is only one "Take Me Out to the Ball Game," then perhaps my first side was not that song, after all.

Then, as my glance strayed from the copies of the disc's inscriptions to the copy of the score of "Take Me Out to the Ball Game," something clicked again. The young woman identified in the now-forgotten verse who is asking her boyfriend to take her to the ballgame—I had assigned her the sign for "female." But there was another sign that appeared on both sides of the disc and in combinations that allowed for both female *and* male activities.

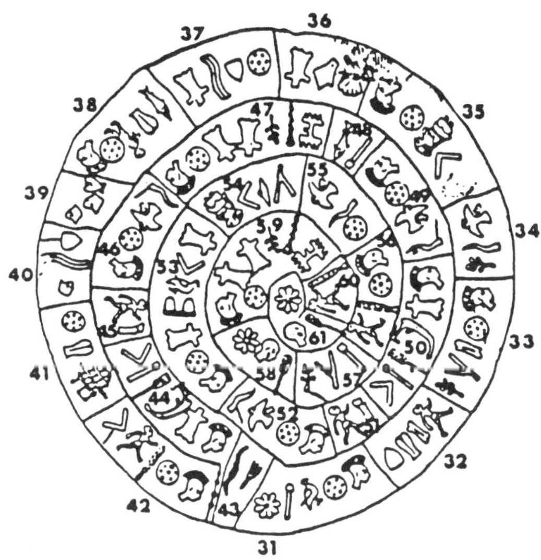

The other side of the Phaestos Disc with an inscription clearly using the basic pictographs of the first side but with several new ones, suggesting a related but different text.

= the crucial pictograph: Casey

= the female Casey: Kitty Casey

= the ball(player) Casey

= unkempt town grid: Mudville?

= sunshine; joy

= fish(y); bad call; "Fraud!"

= axe: "Kill (the umpire)!"

The crucial new vocabulary on the second side of the Phaestos Disc that led to the discovery of the second classic baseball text.

What would happen if I translated this sign with the *proper* name of the young woman and then carried that same name over to the second side?

I tried this, and sure enough—this proper name began to occur with a certain regularity. Other words then began to fall into place—the familiar ones such as "one," "two," "three," "strike," "crowd," "cheer," and such, but also some new ones that now made sense (e.g. the recurrent fish sign that now seemed to read as "fishy" or "fraud"). The test would come with the final box, at the very center of the disc—there could be no forcing that one. And sure enough, there was the sign for the proper name I had been following, but now shorn of his hair—"disgraced"?—and with the already established sign for "strike."

I would not have believed that I could ever surpass the pride and excitement I had felt when I discovered the translation of the first side of the Phaestos Disc. But it was to be. For here was the second side's text clearly confronting me with that crucial name-sign, the equivalent of Ventris's tripod: The name of the heroine of "Take Me Out to the Ball Game" was none other than Kitty Casey, the crucial sign was thus "Casey," and the second side of the

: active (dynamic) ball-player Casey + bat: "Mighty Casey comes to bat."

: dirty town—without joy + crowd + root = inverted Casey: "But there is no joy in Mudville" (due to Casey)

: (departing) joy + hairless (disgraced) Casey + strike: "No joy—(mighty Casey has struck out."

Some translated boxes from the second side of the Phaestos Disc, using the vocabulary deciphered by the author.

Phaestos Disc contains the words—essentially—to "Casey at the Bat." Composed, or so we have been told, in 1888, 20 years before the song that is inscribed on the other side.

From that point on, most of the loose threads extending from the Phaestos Disc mystery pretty much tied themselves off. The full explanation will naturally be published in more specialized journals, but those who have followed the argument this far deserve to be told that "the missing link" has been identified—the one individual capable of bridging the Old World inscription and the New World lyrics: Ernest Lawrence Thayer, reputed author of "Casey at the Bat." Thayer was a Harvard graduate (1885), a man of considerable sophistication; after graduation he went to Paris, where he undoubtedly fell in with a highly cosmopolitan group of people—this was, after all, the Jamesian era for Americans abroad. Meanwhile, it was his classmate William Randolph Hearst who is said to have asked Thayer to contribute a poem to his San Francisco newspaper. Does it seem likely that an expatriate Jamesian Harvard grad in the year 1888 would be able to come up with such a quintessentially "sport" of a poem as "Casey at the Bat"? (Recall that Sterling Dow and John Chadwick describe the text as a "freak.")

What *is* highly likely is that someone who was involved in the removal of the disc from a Cretan site would have approached Thayer in Europe; Thayer's friendship with Hearst would have been common knowledge at a time when Hearst was known to be interested in buying up anything the Old World had for sale; whether Thayer then worked on the translation by himself or with the help of European scholars remains unproven at this time. (Federigo Halbherr's role in all this also remains less than clear: Certainly no one knew both the ancient Cretan and contemporary Continental worlds better than he.) In any case, once Thayer had the text translated, he chose to release the poem from the one side in 1888 in an obscure column in the *San Francisco Examiner* (on June 3). Note, too, that Thayer did not sign his name but used the pen-name "Phin"—clearly a pun on the Phaestos Disc word signed with a fish, meaning "fishy," or "fraud."

Whether Thayer intended this publication as a trial balloon or not—to see, that is, what response he might get from the scholarly community—we may never know. The poem went all but unnoticed until some months later when it was taken up by a popular comedian and singer of the day, William DeWolf Hopper. Soon Hopper was reciting "Casey at the Bat" on every possible occasion. Thayer must have held his breath for some time, wondering if he was going to be exposed (and years later he would write to the *New York Times* about his authorship of this poem, "for this ["Casey"], perhaps the greatest of my sins, I was exclusively to blame"); or perhaps he was scared off by all the attention Hopper's recitations was bringing to the work (Hopper claimed to have recited it over 10,000 times).

In any case, Thayer withheld publication of the text on the other side of the disc until, finally, after 20 years, when it was announced in 1908 that the so-called Phaestos Disc had been "discovered," he felt free to release the translation. (After reading this, Joel Zoss—himself a well-published historian of baseball—called my attention to yet another confirming fact: The special committee set up to decide on the claim that Abner Doubleday had invented baseball released its results in the first days of 1908. By insisting that Doubleday did deserve credit, the report must have made Thayer and anyone else involved in the hoax feel that they were home free.) Back in America by this time, Thayer made contact with Jack Norworth (probably through Hopper's vaudeville network), turned the poem over to him—and the rest is part of all our histories.

Yet some may still question whether Thayer, the sophisticated man here described, would have become involved in all this. But Thayer was a special variety of Harvard sophisticate: he had been the editor of the *Lampoon*, the college humor magazine whose staff has always indulged in more than its share of pranks and hoaxes. Lest this seem forced, consider no less an authority than the philosopher George Santayana, a fellow *Lampoon* editor of Thayer's, writing in his *Persons and Places*:

> The man who gave the tone to the *Lampoon* at that time was Ernest Thayer.... He seemed a man apart, and his wit was not so much jocular as Mercutio-like, curious and whimsical, as if he saw the broken edges of things that appear whole. There was some obscurity in his play with words, and a feeling (which I shared) that the absurd side of things is pathetic. Probably nothing in his later performance may bear out what I have just said of him, because American life was then becoming unfavorable to idiosyncrasies of any sort, and the current smoothed and rounded out all the odd pebbles.

Is this not a perfect description of the individual who would foist off the Minoan texts of "Take Me Out to the Ball Game" and "Casey at the Bat" as indigenous American works?

What will follow from my discovery remains to be seen. I anticipate that a number of previously unidentifiable artifacts from the Minoan world will now yield their secrets as baseball equipment. At the very least there will be a reappraisal of many of the remains and artifacts of the Minoans' culture. Various so-called "cult statues," for instance, may now take on a different significance. Or consider the distinctive courtyards of the great Minoan palaces, which some experts have hitherto claimed were used for the bull-leaping ceremonies: I am now proposing that they were more likely the "ballparks" and I believe that rechecking their measurements will confirm this.

Meanwhile, other scholars of this period and region will undoubtedly be compelled to look into other possible ramifications of this discovery. I myself lack the specialized linguistic knowledge to proceed very far with original texts, but I have had a brief chance to look through some of the secondary sources. R. F. Willetts, for instance, one of the leading authorities on the ancient Cretan world, has this to say (in *The Civilization of Ancient Crete*, Univ. of California Press, 1977) about the findings of still another recognized expert, Sinclair Hood and his survey of the Minoan scripts:

> The discovery of comparable signs [i.e. to the Minoans'] on pottery at Tordos in Rumania, at Troy, on Melos, and in Egypt had already at the beginning of this century produced a widespread belief that a single system of writing had developed at an early period throughout this area. It now begins to look as if this belief, apparently fantastic, might not be entirely unfounded. . . . Some of the signs are like the signs on Trojan pots and whorls; and beehive-like huts on stilts have been compared with a sign on the Phaestos Disc.

The last-mentioned sign happens to be the one that translates so consistently as "ballpark" in my rendering, and although it may be premature—and I am in no way suggesting that Willetts or Hood are yet prepared to go this far with me—I am prepared to surmise that what we have here are a series of ballparks throughout the greater Mediterranean world—in effect, a Bronze Age major league.

Meanwhile, I am testing my new glossary with other Minoan

inscriptions. My current challenge is a text found on a stone block at Mallia, the third of the great Minoan palaces. A number of the same signs as those on the Phaestos Disc can be identified, including the crucial one for "Casey." It appears to be yet another poem or song, but at the moment I'm stuck with a line that would seem to read, "Casey [is] dancing [with] a yellow red-berry"—and clearly this doesn't make sense.

As for the Phaestos Disc and its inscriptions, I think the last word should be given to Sterling Dow and John Chadwick, certainly the most unprejudiced, and now prescient, authorities one could ask for: "Beset with doubts, qualifications, and difficulties, the Disc is almost unreal, and only the fact that it was found by an excavator in an excavation compels its acceptance." Clearly, the disc is now more real—and it is the excavator who is now "beset with doubts." But I can only feel blessed to have been the first to come across these two texts, and if it is not an endorsement of the freelancer's approach, perhaps it is proof that the gods have been watching over our national pastime for longer than we realize.

Was Casey a Canuck?

By BILL FITSELL

EVER SINCE A YOUNG, bewhiskered, New York fireman by the name of Alexander Cartwright converted "town ball and rounders" into a four-based game in 1845, Americans have engaged in a year-round love affair with the summer sport of "base ball."

They have warmed to the game's lore, its legends, and particularly to its larrupers—the larger-than-life young men who lambaste the horsehide (now cowhide) ball over the fence for a base-clearing home run.

More than a century after baseball's invention in the United States, Canada is threatening to take half or all of the World Series games beyond American borders. The Montreal Expos and the Toronto Blue Jays, their line-ups laden with American-born players, may return an insult now commonplace in hockey: the Stanley Cup finals of Canada's national game being fought in American cities.

If the impossible, an all-Canadian World Series, should happen some October, might it add insult to injury to restate the age old query: "Would the real Casey please stand up?" and to answer: "He's a real flesh-and-blood Canadian!"

Yes, born and bred in Ontario, within a morning's horse and buggy ride of Kingston, where baseball has been played since before hockey was invented.

Ah, but then, I'm ahead of myself. Time for some warm-up pitches.

Casey at the Bat, the classic ballad by Ernest Lawrence Thayer (1863-1940) was, of course, about a fictional character, Mighty Casey, who left Mudville fans in misery by fanning with two out in the ninth inning and the tying runs on base. Since the poem was first published in the *San Francisco Examiner* in 1888 and popularized on the stage by Dewitt Hopper, baseball enthusiasts have never stopped enjoying the epic lines or guessing the identity of the real Casey.

The poet's Casey has been immortalized for striking out even while baseball's greats are remembered for *not* striking out—Ty Cobb, Babe Ruth, Mickey Mantle, Ted Williams, Jackie Robinson, Hank Aaron, and so on.

Reared on Frank Merriwell heroes and Hollywood endings, the U.S. public clamored for a baseball ballad that ended on a winning note: Twenty years after Casey left "no joy in Mudville" he and the fans got their revenge. Revered sports writer Grantland Rice redeemed the fallen hero by composing an ode that finished:

Oh! somewhere in this favored land
dark clouds may hide the sun,
And somewhere bands no longer
play and children have no fun;
And somewhere over blighted
loves there hangs a heavy pall,
But Mudville hearts are happy
now—for Casey hit the ball.

The American dream of success notwithstanding, this version has long been forgotten. Baseball aficionados, familiar with the ups and downs in the real and imaginary innings of life, preferred Thayer's ending, with the mighty Casey fanning the air in failure. As the author told his Harvard class of 1885 at a turn-of-the-century homecoming: "We have found that playing the game is very different from watching it played and that splendid theories, even when accepted by the combatants, are apt to be lost sight of in the confusion of active battle."

The poem has become, said poet-anthologist Louis Untermeyer, "the acknowledged classic of baseball, its anthem and theme song." Subtitled *A Ballad of the Republic*, the original 52-line poem carried when first published the nom de plume, "Phin," one of Thayer's nicknames at Harvard . As is the case with the identification of the *real* Casey, many impostors stepped forward as the poem's creator, but the originator finally won out.

Hopper, a comic opera star, and later husband of Hollywood columnist Hedda Hopper (and father of Paul Drake of TV's *Perry Mason*), made the poem famous through 10,000 performances. With his deep voice and exaggerated gestures, he celebrated the combined humor and irony of the poem and maintained the suspense to the last line.

In 1945, a moustachioed Casey was brought to life by Walt Disney in an animated film entitled *Make Mine Music*. Seven years later, the Mighty Casey took his cuts in an operetta. Its composers stuck to the traditional story line, but other writers have not.

In 1979 the debate over who the real Casey was reached the 13th session of the Court of Historic Appeals in San Francisco. New evidence was presented to show that the poem was based on a real-life occurrence in Stockton, California, in 1888. Ignoring other evidence that Thayer was back in his native New England at the time, *Sporting News* columnist Leonard Koppett, Watergate style, produced an 18-line "erasure" from the original poem that pointed to Casey's involvement with gambling: He thus threw the game by striking out.

Former *Globe and Mail* sports columnist Alan Abel, in his book *But I Loved It Plenty Well* (1983), took the ridiculous one step further by revealing that Casey was strung out on cocaine.

Now is the time to inject a serious note: The Canadian facts about the original Casey, the baseball player who once inspired a Kingston journalist to write poetically—not by striking out but by hitting a towering shot (foul, as it turned out), and then taking a base on balls!

His name was Orrin Robinson Casey, born on Casey's Point, near Carnahan's Bay or Perch Cove in the Hay Bay area of

Adolphustown, where a century later the farm boys were still playing baseball "come hell or high water or the haying done." He grew up and played baseball at Newburgh, the village that once vied with nearby Napanee for the county seat of Lennox and Addington.

Lest any American reader spill his beer or Cracker Jacks over the revelation that Casey was a Canadian, first consider his lineage. He was the seventh-generation survivor of a certain Thomas Casey who was rescued as a child during the Irish riots in Ulster three centuries ago, grew up in England and later emigrated to America. His several-times-over grandfather, Samuel Casey, made his mark on 18th-century silverware in Little Rest (now Kingston), Rhode Island. Samuel's children were American Loyalists who came to Upper Canada via Vermont in the late 1780s. The Casey clan became farmers, millers, members of parliament, doctors and journalists.

Some of the pioneer Canadian Caseys were indeed known for their might. Samuel Casey, Jr. represented the "uppity" Fourth-towners of Adolphustown in a wrestling challenge match with the residents of the fifth township of Marysburgh in Prince Edward County. Sam threw his opponent and the Fourth-towners retained their superior attitude.

Our 19th-century hero, O.R. (Bob) Casey went on to a 20-year professional baseball career in Syracuse, New York, and Detroit, Michigan, but was apparently overlooked in the recent "Who's Casey?" debate because of an unexplained error in *The Official Encyclopedia of Baseball* published in 1959. His record with the Detroit Wolverines of the National Association was combined with that of another Casey, Dennis Patrick, a weak-hitting outfielder from Binghamton, New York, who was also considered in the guesswork to discover the real Casey.

Although he played only nine games at third base and second base in Detroit, the record of Canada's Casey reveals that he had the credentials to be the inspiration for the poem. *The Baseball Encyclopedia* (Macmillan), which correctly listed Bob Casey's big-league record, depicted him as a man with the physical stature of the mighty fellow who took two called strikes and missed the third. He stood five feet, 11 inches and weighed 190 pounds, whereas most of the Detroit regulars were in the five-foot, six-inch range and tipped the scales in the 138- to 170-pound bracket.

But it is his playing record that conjures up visions of *Casey at the Bat*. His batting average of .231—nine hits in 39 trips to the plate—was disappointing; but he hit for extra bases—two doubles, a triple and a homer—and compiled a slugging average of .410, much higher than his regular teammates.

Home runs were scarce in the dead-ball years before *Casey at the Bat* was written. In 1882, Detroit hit 20 of the league's 126, and the league leader, the Wolverines's George (Dandy) Wood, won the circuit long-ball crown with seven in 84 games. The evidence, however, is that teammate Bob Casey, despite his reputation as a slugger, never walked once and struck out 15 out of 39 times!

Percentages are as much a part of baseball as hot dogs and scorecards. But these figures may or may not reveal why Casey was relegated to the minor leagues. The stats do not explain why the 1973 publication, *Who's Who in Professional Baseball*, tagged Daniel Maurice Casey, a pitcher, as the much-feared Casey of the poem. One of four Caseys who played baseball in the 1880s, he was a pitcher with a lifetime batting average of .162!

Strangely enough, another baseball expert, George Gipe, author of *The Great American Sports Book* (published in 1978) blithely discounted Canada's entry in the Casey sweepstakes. "Hardly a slugger," he said of Orrin Robinson (Bob) Casey, looking at his one home run in 39 trips but ignoring the fact that the Babe Ruth of the era, Dandy Woods, clouted only seven in 375 trips or one in every 53 trips.

Gipe, however, made one comment that keeps Canada's Casey in contention and may keep the guessing game going for another century: "The author asserted several times before his demise in 1935 that he based the poem on no particular character or athlete. That may or may not be true, for we cannot discount the subconscious in these matters."

Bob Casey himself, in an interview with *The New York Times* a few years before his death in 1936, readily admitted that he often struck out with the bases loaded and two men out. "When Hopper began reciting Casey and everyone in Syracuse pointed me out as the hero, I let them build me up," he said. "I was playing on a semi-professional team in Syracuse [when the poem was published] and it is not likely that a young man out at Harvard ever heard of me." On another occasion, however, he was reported to have become irritated when actor Hopper agreed with the author that no living baseball player was the subject of his poem.

Another time-out, sports fans. Consider this new evidence from Canada. I submit a clipping from *The British Whig*, the newspaper that merged in 1926 with the *Kingston Standard*. It is dated October 15, 1885, and features a front-page report of a game played in Kingston's Cricket Field between the hometown Park Nine Baseball Club and the team from Newburgh, a village once called not Mudville but Rogue's Hollow. Soundly thumped 20 to 6 in a previous game in Newburgh, the visiting team was strengthened by "Casey of the Syracuse club," who was home for the winter.

"He is a heavy fellow, with cool head and sinewy arms," wrote *The Whig* reporter. "He was dubbed 'Jumbo' and played third base quite acceptably."

The scene was set. Seventh inning. The score tied 11-11. "Casey spat upon his hands, grabbed a piece of maple, tapped the plate and awaited the delivery of the ball. It came, it was his time, and with a MIGHTY swipe, he lifted it high into the air.

"Old baseballers gazed at it as it soared up and curved away above the trees and came down with a thud beyond Park Avenue (Bagot Street). It took two throws of a lively baseballer to bring it back to the pitcher's box. The strike was 'foul,' but it showed the [Kingston] team what a batter they had to deal with. A dozen men say they never saw such a 'sky-rocket' before."

Afterwards, the reporter added, Casey walked, and in the eighth inning Kingston scored two runs and Casey flied to center with two men on. Newburgh, as did Mudville, lost—13-11.

Now, how could this newspaper article have had any influence on a newly graduated Harvard student in Boston?, the baseball court might ask.

Well, Your Honor, the prolific Caseys of Canada, the two original Loyalists, each had 10 children and their offspring were everywhere. Thomas Willet Casey, a relative of Bob Casey, was editor and publisher of *The Napanee Express* and his son, Willet F. Casey, was associated with *The Boston Globe*. There's the circumstantial link. And don't forget, the reference to the subconscious.

When Orrin Robinson Casey died November 28, 1936, in Syracuse, the *Sunday Herald* reported that he had recalled a specific case of striking out with the bases loaded in a hard-fought game between Detroit and Minneapolis.

But did Casey strike out in the game of life?

No. As a general store salesman along the old Erie Canal, he witnessed many acts of cruelty committed against mules pulling the canal boats. He spoke out and, as a result, the Central New York Society for the Prevention of Cruelty to Animals was formed and he served as its superintendent for 45 years. In fact, he died on the job at 77, after investigating an alleged case of mistreatment of horses exposed to bitter weather in a farm field.

The *Napanee Beaver* reported that "Casey at the Bat died at Home in Syracuse" and pointed out, along with his birthplace in Adolphustown, his former residency in Newburgh. The Kingston *Whig's* headline was the inevitable: "Mighty Casey Has Struck Out!" The article mentioned that his father was Hiram Weeks Casey, who died in Kingston in 1903.

According to the obituary, Bob Casey's closest survivor was his sister, Emma L. Casey, widow of former Kingston mayor and wholesale grocer, Robert J. Carson. One of the latter's four sons was named Orrin A. Carson, who became professor of metallurgy at Queen's University and served on the university's Athletic Board of Control for 42 years until his death in 1964. The name Orrin lives on through Dr. Carson's son, Robert Orrin Carson of Fontill, Ontario, who prizes among his family heirlooms a silver flask handed down from his uncle, Orrin Robinson Casey. It is engraved with the initials, O.R.C.—which a Canadian baseball fan might say stands for "Our Real Casey."

This is all insufficient evidence perhaps for Adolphustown or Newburgh to erect a sign: "Home of Casey at the Bat," but surely plenty enough for Bob Casey to be recognized by the Canadian Baseball Hall of Fame.

Baseball and The Urban Crisis

By JAMES KISSANE

IN ST. LOUIS, some people say the reason that city experienced no major riot in the summer of 1967 was that Lou Brock was having a good year. Through the hot summer, while Newark and Detroit were torn by violence and other cities across the country writhed or cringed, the Cardinals stayed ahead in the pennant race, even when their ace pitcher, Bob Gibson, broke his leg, then they beat the Red Sox in an unusually exciting World Series. Brock was crucial, but so were Curt Flood and, when his leg mended, the superb Gibson. When I first heard the relatively peaceful St. Louis summer attributed to the Cardinals and their black stars, I asked, "What about Detroit?" The Tigers were hot for the American League championship right up to the last day of the season, but that hadn't kept the city cool. "Yes, but Willie Horton was the Tigers' only Negro standout in '67," I was reminded, "and he got hurt and couldn't play."

Maybe, especially since racial justice and civil violence are such serious matters, this kind of roll-your-own sociology can appeal only to baseball fans, who are terrible sentimentalists anyway. St. Louis has had more than its share of problems, and a winning ball team won't solve or even conceal them. Yet if even a hypochondriac can be sick, so may a sentimentalist have a glimpse of honest truth. Our games *are* important to us, though not always in the ways or for the reasons we suppose. We can easily make connections between the Olympic Games and the quality of Greek civilization, between gladiatorial combats and the callous brutality of imperial Rome, between Britain's habit of winning wars and the playing fields of Eton. Perhaps it is no less reasonable to link the fortunes of that sport we fulsomely call Our National Pastime to the fate of our nation's cities. Major League baseball naturally shares the problems of the great cities that support it; I'd go further and say that the state of the game furnishes a vivid clue to the condition of urban life.

To most people who love the national pastime it seems clear that, despite what attendance figures, television coverage, and players' salaries might indicate, baseball these days is drying up at the roots and withering at the top. Even the hyper-organized Little Leagues are a bad sign: a genteel suburban takeover of a proletarian sport that really belongs to the city sandlots and the country cow pastures. I don't suppose either Babe Ruth or Satchel Paige would have made it in the Little Leagues: Who would have driven them over to their practices? As for the Minor Leagues, which old-timers think of as the nerve and sinew of the game, they are in sorry shape. And the multiplying Major League franchises remind me of the way some trees seem to bear seeds in crazy abundance just before they die. Remember the Miracle of Milwaukee? In Kansas City they went about as far as they could go.

I called baseball proletarian, which is surely what it is, compared with the sports of football and golf. Football, of course, was nurtured on the privileged turf of college campuses, and though it's lost the boola-boola raccoon-coat pep-rally flavor, it still means wicker picnic baskets out of the back ends of station wagons, though beer has replaced the cocktails. The pro game brings Fat Cats into the cities from way out, and they sit huddled in stadium coats with hand-warmers and field glasses. Golf, for those who can afford the time and money, is a nice way to get outdoors, though it has become pretty much a pastoral extension of the businessman's lunch, taken up for impure reasons by people who would really rather have a Buick. As a spectator sport, golf lacks nearly all the essentials: no spectacle, only very incidental ritual, and no real sense of community. The belligerence, discipline, and fidelity of an army—Arnie's or anyone else's—are no substitute for the festive unruliness of a proper audience.

It's easy to understand why baseball has lost ground in the 60s. The sports fan then hoped to appease restless isolation and boredom with whatever could promise a few spasmodic thrills between TV commercials. It's a slow-paced game, whose appeal is not to the spectator looking for action but to one who needs a breather. Its highest moments—almost wholly lost on television—are performed with languid detachment and even contemptuous ease (watch a double play) rather than with frenzied abandon or grim concentration. So much of the fan's pleasure in baseball is in its *ambience*: What happens takes place so decisively in a context. At its best the game is incorporate with cigar smoke and the warm afternoon sun, with cold beer and gaudy signs painted on the outfield walls, with the cries of the hawkers and the comforting sound of the ball smacking into the catcher's mitt as the starting pitcher loosens up on the sidelines. There is also what you would have to call the *historical* context, sometimes unjustly ridiculed as the "folklore" of the game. For the real fan—more, surely, than in other sports—the past is present at a ball game: what the batter did last time up, what his season's average is up to that moment, how many homers he hit last summer, what Paul Waner or Charlie Gehringer once did in a similar situation, how DiMaggio would have moved back to take that fly. An afternoon at the ballpark isn't only about *now*; it's about *then*. The beauty of the game is that it's so haunted.

I mention all this to suggest that baseball in the 70s became an anachronism, just as the cities are today. And what baseball has been to the cities, our sprawling ex-urban culture can't use, or doesn't know it needs. But Marshall McLuhan, as usual, got here first. Baseball, he said, is "the elegant, abstract image of an industrial society living by split-second timing" and hence has lost its relevance in our electronic and computerized society. Football—non-positional, decentralized—has shouldered baseball to the periphery of American life in the 60s.

But I'm more nostalgic (and less optimistic) than McLuhan, so he hasn't said it all for me. Just as baseball brings the past into the present, so it has connected the city and the country. Cooperstown was just a hamlet, I suppose, when Abner Doubleday fictitiously invented the game there in 1839. I imagine, too, that it struck the first city slickers who watched it like the sort of game that would have been invented by a guy named Abner. A Major League ballpark still has a kind of poignant incongruity about it: a cow pasture in the Bronx, a village square fitted into the round peg of a double-tiered arena. And the career of a major leaguer was almost always a link between rural and urban America: Carl Hubbell, Ty Cobb, Deacon Law, Shoeless Joe Jackson, Dizzy and Paul Dean—country bumpkins who did their stuff for New York, Detroit, Pittsburgh, Chicago, and St. Louis. Or, on the other hand, a young ballplayer born in the shadow of Ebbetts Field usually had to get back there by way of Salinas or Joplin or St. Cloud, so that a farmer's boy and the delicatessen owner's son might copy the wind-up or strain for the autograph of the same left-handed pitcher. My father and my grandfather both saw a lot of baseball in their time: my father mostly in Cincinnati and Cleveland and my grandfather in semi-pro leagues in Iowa and South Dakota. That was almost the only thing they had in common, but they had watched some of the same ballplayers at different points in their careers and could always have a good time talking about that. I think it significant that two writers who are eloquent about baseball (in their different ways) should be John Updike and Bernard Malamud: an elegist of rural and smalltown America, and a great urban fabulist.

Maybe it was its atmosphere of fusion—sights and smells, past and present, country and city—that made baseball in its heyday something of a rejuvenating daily rite that transformed the metropolis into a neighborhood. No wonder it has never really appealed to fancy people; my idea of the authentic baseball crowd is a lot of men—janitors, bus drivers, night watchmen—who have an afternoon free to sit in the sun in their undershirts away from a job that isn't much and an apartment full of kids that is too much. And night games, though that's about all there are now, never seem quite genuine. Floodlights and darkness give too much focus and blot out the ambience. Night baseball, they say, saved the game.

But it saved it pretty much the way television saved the movies.

I believe if someone had been paying attention to what was happening to baseball he could have foreseen what has become of the cities. Perhaps, too, if we had looked after baseball, it might even have made some difference. When the Dodgers left Brooklyn for Los Angeles, everyone—not just the Bums' fans—should have recognized a social tragedy. It was a kind of civic heart transplant from a living and hence needy donor to a recipient that would have thrived no worse on a second Disneyland. Of course one mustn't idealize baseball. Sometimes the management treats the players like children; sometimes the players' actions would make that comparison an affront to childhood. Managers are abused by fans and sloughed off by owners. Like the cities themselves, the sport has been at worst shamefully racist and at best insensitive to the problems of its blacks.

Yet this old-fashioned game, played in clothes from a forgotten era, can still assert—from time to time—its special power against contrariety. Compared to 1967, 1968 was a good summer in Detroit; there were no massive disturbances, and the Tigers did not falter. After an improbable victory over the Cardinals in the World Series, Detroit experienced a moment of amity rare for that turbulent city and unique in this season of national urban distress. At the height of the celebration a Detroit cop threw his arms around a black fellow townsman with a greeting of "Soul Brother!" Nor did the black man take offense at the white policeman's use of that privileged password, as he might have, but returned it with the same jubilation. Stock-car racing doesn't affect people this way; I don't believe football or golf really do either.

Of course it's sentimental to value such an incident; it hardly weighs against that other one at the Algiers Motel. And as for the Tigers and their followers, the balm of euphoria works no lasting cure. Maybe the white cop and the black fan were forgotten in Detroit the first time Gates Brown struck out pinch-hitting for Al Kaline or when Mayo Smith sent Earl Wilson to the showers too soon. But if so, that would only be a measure of our own cynicism and bad faith and no telling mark against a game that gives us, on the diamond and in the streets, some moments of real grace.

This essay was written in 1968.

The New Mythopoeism of Baseball: W.P. Kinsella's Baseball Fiction

By THOMAS L. ALTHERR

PERHAPS NO OTHER American sport has resisted simple, pat explanations for its appeal as has baseball. Attempting to explain why a boys' game (one part anachronism, one part business, one part pure repetition) should have lasted so long in American hearts has caused many enthusiasts and critics alike to scratch their heads. Normally articulate persons fumble for words to elucidate their passion, ending often in a typical admission: "I don't know, I just love it." Other sports bid fiercely for their share of fan revenue and allegiance, but they have had a tough time dislodging baseball from its preeminence as the national pastime. Rail as one might about greedy owners and players, the commodification of baseball cards and paraphernalia, and other adulterations, the game remains. Surviving third league challenges, strikes, scandals, racial friction, drugs, the designated hitter, and artificial turf, baseball blossoms forth innocently each spring.

For some, the game has been a reminder of America's rural past, a welcome (or not-so-welcome) relic of premechanized countrysides, lazy pastoral picnics, a surfeit of rustic peace. For others it has been the opposite, the game that grew up with the cities, assimilated immigrants, and matched the hustle and bustle of industrialism. Some interpreters have combined these two, preferring to see baseball, especially the park and stadium, as green oases in gray cities. There are those who suggest that baseball is now the suburban game, drawing its players increasingly from thousands of past Little Leaguers. At times, the sport has seemed a leisure-time reflection of mechanical perfection, the well-oiled team with its smooth Tinker-to-Evers-to-Chance teamwork, even reminiscent of Civil War military organization. Yet others have asserted that baseball's value lies in its opposition to routinized mechanical modes of work, as a recuperative blend full of whim, fancy, flukes, and other unpredictabilities. For the former, baseball has been the game of inches; for the latter, the game without time. More modern sport sociologists and historians have offered depictions of baseball as a mirror of deep-seated American values; positive ones such as individual effort, hard work, equal opportunity, cooperative achievement, moral role-modeling, and community pride, and negative ones such as over-competitiveness, racist exclusion, sexism, swaggering machoism, jingoism, and narcissistic self-indulgence. Even when not presenting a pretty face, baseball has been something for everyone.

The plentitude of these theories should not be surprising. Indeed baseball often pitches us onto paradoxes. It is a pretechnological game which survives economically in modern America thanks to the wonders of electronics. It is among the cheapest of mass entertainments, yet players have the highest average salary. Despite decades of racial segregation, many non-white players have flourished since the late 1940s, establishing several key career records.

Structurally baseball has its oddities. Theoretically unbounded in time and space, the sport does conform to temporal and spatial limits. Foul lines might extend forever and teams stay up at bat into the future, but there are outfield fences and attempts to speed up the game. Field dimensions have stayed relatively constant, but the game has witnessed, some say suffered, numerous gimmicks and glitzy alterations to keep up with "the times".

As if these paradoxes were not taxing enough, baseball is inherently a very new and a very old game. Dressing up in snappy miracle-fabric uniforms, playing on artificial or highly manicured grass fields under the glare of lights and neon scoreboards at night, and mouthing neologisms straight from the computer age, today's players fit a fast-paced lifestyle. Some are more likely to worry about their investment portfolios, endorsement contracts, or agent's negotiations than their batting and earned run averages. Managers and coaches rely increasingly on computer statistics and projections to make what were formerly intuitive decisions. The game has always been rife with statistics, but many fans have come to overemphasize the numbers side of the game, sometimes even substituting computer games for the real thing. To satisfy more restless fans, team organizations offer promotional attractions not always related to the game on the field. With more than a grain of truth, many baseball purists and old-timers find the present version of baseball alien to their memories of a slower day with more dedicated players and more seats-of-their-pants managers.

And yet for all its modernisms, hype, and hoopla, baseball is an old game, old in the context of American experience and, as some myth critics would argue, an ancient game. Historians have not been able to pinpoint when baseball changed officially from rounders and other folk games, but they have found references to baseball-like games as early as 1744. Colonial Americans had the same propensities to play a circular game that did not involve person-to-person contact, territorial gain, or placing a ball or other projectile in a hoop, goal, or basket. The game probably conformed much more to the common agrarian rhythms of those times, the circularity of seasons, days, and hours, the repetitiveness of agricultural tasks and phases. Every farmer was aware of time, to be sure, but it was sidereal, astronomical time, not industrial, linear time. Some myth critics and novelists have pushed this time connection back even further. Although they don't suggest that baseball existed in ancient societies in a format recognizable to modern Americans, these writers have argued that baseball has assumed and incorporated many of the archetypal patterns of the past. Some have found intriguing parallels to older quest or holy grail searches, to life cycle and aging phases, to resurrection stories, to immortality wishes, to fertility rituals, to Armageddon-like clashes, to personal super-human heroic feats of strength and endurance, to tales of the suspension of time, to shamanistic trickster narratives, to pilgrimage patterns, to sanctification ceremonies, and to other various forms of preagrarian and preindustrial magic. Several have come very close to presenting baseball as a religion that subsumes all or many of the functions of "regular" religions, a not-so-profane set of beliefs and rituals, replete with player-priests, manager-bishops, umpire-acolytes, and fan-congregations.

A few modern American novelists, notably Bernard Malamud, Mark Harris, Philip Roth, Robert Coover, and, in a less serious vein, George Plimpton, have delved into these archetypal themes, clothing them in baseball plots. Indeed many readers have come to expect that most modern "baseball" novels are not going to be faithful literary transcriptions of the game itself, but rather explorations of some over-arching human experience. Probably the novelist who has established this expectation the firmest is W. P. Kinsella, a Canadian writer who has claimed the accolade "baseball novelist". First coming to the attention of the literary world with his short stories about western Canadian Indian life, Kinsella reached a larger audience with his 1982 novel *Shoeless Joe*, which won the Houghton Mifflin Literary Fellowship Award. Following that success, Kinsella has published another novel, *The Iowa Baseball Confederacy* (1986) and two collections of baseball-oriented short stories, *The Thrill of the Grass* (1984) and *The Further Adventures of Slugger McBatt* (1988).[1] In each of these works, Kinsella has posited that baseball is much more than the surface game, that it corresponds to a series of ingrained human aspirations. Relentlessly Kinsella has broken away from conventional time, stereotypical characters, and plausible occurrences to place baseball before his readers as the truest religion, the magical salvation of moderns. Of course, given Kinsella's occasional excesses, the reader might justly suspect him of satire and parody. But the prevalent tone of his writing is clearly reverential at the great cathedral of baseball. Surely that is the interpretation Phil Alden Robinson chose when he adapted *Shoeless Joe* into his 1989 film *Field of Dreams*.

Shoeless Joe, familiar to many readers even before *Field of Dreams*, concerns Iowa farmer Ray Kinsella's repeated muted epiphanies instructing him first to build a baseball field to bring to life Shoeless Joe Jackson and, as it turns out, other 1919 White Sox barred from baseball, next to kidnap recluse writer J. D. Salinger to lead him to some mysterious fortune in Iowa, and then to travel to northern Minnesota to grant "Moonlight" Graham the chance to fulfill his aborted dream of hitting in the major leagues. Finally Ray comes face to face with his lost twin brother and, more importantly, his father, Johnny Kinsella, with whom Ray had never had a solid rapport before his death. Despite these events, implausible to the rational mind, *Shoeless Joe* succeeds as a literary tour de force. The dreamy, disarming qualities of the plot and the prose draw the reader into Ray's quest as if it were one's own destiny. As writer Daniel Okrent remarked in a popular review: "Mr. Kinsella is drunk on the complementary elixirs, literature and baseball, and the cocktail he mixes of the two is a lyrical, seductive and altogether winning concoction."[2]

The Iowa Baseball Confederacy, however, is a less successful effort, despite its extra doses of black humor. Suffering from a more inchoate plot, especially in the late chapters, the novel details the protagonist Gideon Clarke's search for evidence about a turn-of-the-century Iowa baseball league whose all-stars played the Chicago Cubs in 1908. Following up on his father's nearly life-consuming obsession to prove the existence of the Confederacy, eventually Gideon locates a "crack" in time and travels back to 1908 Onamata, Iowa, then known as the Big Inning. There he and his friend, Stan Rogalski, witness an incredible forty-day 2,614-inning marathon baseball duel between the Cubs and the all-stars, which takes place while a flood sweeps the town away. President Teddy Roosevelt arrives to take his cut at the plate and to persuade the Cubs to return to Chicago (because their second-stringers have dropped the team into the second division). After that intrusion, reminiscent of E. L. Doctorow's *Ragtime*, Kinsella makes his plot even more ludicrous. Leonardo da Vinci appears by time machine and claims to have invented baseball. As for Gideon, he also falls in love with a local lady, gets entangled with a gigantic trickster Indian, and ponders the bittersweet position in which time travel has placed him. He returns to the present, dazed at his impotence to change the past. Reviewer Eliot Asinof was justified when he complained about these fantastic leaps, that Kinsella "teases us with an assortment of crooked pitches," but for all of that, *The Iowa Baseball Confederacy* has its brilliant segments which remind the reader of the enchantment of baseball.[3]

Space prohibits any full-length discussion of the individual pieces in the two short story collections, *The Thrill of the Grass* and *The Further Adventures of Slugger McBatt*, but three stories merit comment. "How I Got My Nickname" from the first collection is a charming retelling of the Bobby Thomson home run saga of 1951, this time with the narrator, Kinsella himself fictionalized, intervening to make sure Thomson gets his at bat. "The Thrill of the Grass," the signature story, resembles *Shoeless Joe* in its tone and ghostliness. Set during the protracted baseball strike of 1981, the plot involves a fan who takes his revenge by engineering the secret replacement of the artificial turf at the nearby stadium with sod, which like-minded fans deliver as sacred offerings. "Distances," in the second collection, returns to Gideon Clarke and Stan Rogalski, who as members of a lackluster town ball team encounter a stranger, Roger Cash, an aging pitcher who promises to lead the team to victory and gambling winnings. Cash proves good on his word, but only, as Gideon finds out, by altering the distance from the mound to home plate to sixty-one feet secretly at night.

What have these rather odd literary products to do with more noble, hoary mythic themes? Taken all together, the novels and short stories might be seen as nothing more than the fanciful ramblings of a fictioneer. Nothing could be more mistaken. Homages to the interior life of baseball and testaments to its mythic and even religious qualities, Kinsella's fiction demands serious attention. He is very cognizant of the tradition of baseball lore, of the ancient connections of the sport, and of its closeness to religious feelings. Although in a 1987 interview he expressed bemusement with LitCrit types who overanalyze his fiction, Kinsella showed that he was aware of his fictional purposes. Discussing the fact that baseball is an "open" game compared to most other sports, which are "twice enclosed," he admitted: "This openness makes for larger than life characters, for mythology."[4]

In terms of traditional baseball lore, Kinsella capitalizes on the emotional connotations of the Shoeless Joe Jackson scandal. The recent Pete Rose gambling controversy might cloud the current reader's judgment, but in 1982, Kinsella has his characters stump for Jackson's exoneration, if not in the eyes of the Hall of Fame, then by resurrecting him on an Iowa corn field. Similarly, references to the Chicago Cubs and New York Giants in *Shoeless Joe* display concrete knowledge of the era. In other books, Kinsella shows similar familiarity with baseball lore. In *The Iowa Baseball Confederacy*, there appears a character named Little Walter, a midget character reminiscent of James Thurber's Pearl Monville in "You Could Look It Up" and Bill Veeck's Eddie Gaedel. In this story, however, Little Walter is not so lucky; he dies from a purposeful pitch (*IBC*, 264). The plot of "How I Got My Nickname" depends heavily on the reader's memory of the 1951 Giants and Bobby Thomson. And "The Last Pennant Before Armageddon" in *The Thrill of the Grass* plays directly off Cub fans' continuing frustration in search of a pennant.

Not only does Kinsella draw upon baseball lore, he considers baseball the perfect game in and of itself and for linking up parts of the American past with the present. He approvingly quotes Salinger's Seymour Glass that baseball is "perhaps the most heart-rending, delicious sport in the Western Hemisphere" (*SB*, 31). Later in *Shoeless Joe*, after watching an astounding play, Ray Kinsella remarks, "The play reaffirms what I already know—that baseball is the most perfect of games, solid, true, pure and precious as diamonds. If only life were so simple. I have often thought, if only there was a framework to life, rules to live by" (*SB*, 78). In *The Iowa Baseball Confederacy*, Drifting Away, the Indian trickster, comments on the game:

> "Baseball is the only single thing the white man has done right."...
>
> "But baseball has solid lines, like so much of what

> the white man makes," I say to him, "and diamonds are close to squares."
>
> "Think of the circles instead of the lines—the ball, the circumference of the bat, the outfield running to the circle of the horizon, the batter running around the bases. Baseball is as close to the circle of perfection as white men are allowed to approach." (*IBC*, 166-7).

When Leonardo da Vinci appears and claims to have invented the game, Stan Rogalski concurs, "It figures. Who else could come up with such perfect dimensions?" (*IBC*, 240)

Everything about baseball drives Kinsella to rhapsody. In *Shoeless Joe*, Ray Kinsella tingles "as if looking forward to a first date," as he constructs the field, and once he has decided he must kidnap Salinger, he vows to feed him baseball intravenously: "I'll pierce a vein and feed him the sounds, smells, and sights of baseball until he tingles with the same magic that enchants me" (*SJ*, 28,34). In his soliloquy, Joe Jackson speaks for Kinsella, too: "I'd wake in the night with the smell of the ballpark in my nose and the cool of the grass on my feet. The thrill of the grass . . . I loved the game. I'd have played for food money. I'd have played free and worked for food . . . I'd play for the Devil's own team just for the touch of a baseball. Hell, I'd play in the dark if I had to" (*SJ*, 12-14). Freedom from time and space constraints is equally appealing. Ray Kinsella notes that on the baseball field "the sense of urgency that governs most lives is pushed to one side like junk mail shoved to the back of a desk" (*SJ*, 73). Gideon Clarke's father, Matthew, raves in *The Iowa Baseball Confederacy* about the limitless expanse of the baseball field: "There's no place in America that's not part of a major-league outfield: the meanest ghetto, the highest point of land, the Great Lakes, the Colorado River. Hell, there's no place in the *world* that's not part of a baseball field" (*IBC*, 41). How could such a game fail to stimulate the nostalgia Salinger details:

> The memories will be so thick that the outfielders will have to brush them away from their faces; squarish

> cars parked around a frame schoolhouse, blankets covering the engine blocks; Christmas carols drifting like tinseled birds toward the golden wash of Northern Lights; women shelling peas in linoleum-floored kitchens, cradling the unshelled pods in brindled aprons, tearing open corn husks and waiting for the thrill of the cool sweet scent; apple-cheeked children and collie dogs, the coffee-and-oil smell of a general store; people gliding over the snow in an open cutter; the dazzling smell of horsehide blankets teasing the senses (*SJ*, 212-213).

For Kinsella baseball will supply a sustaining measure of constancy and connection with the past. Again Salinger exclaims:

> I don't have to tell you that the one constant through all the years has been baseball. America has been erased like a blackboard, only to be rebuilt and then erased again. But baseball has marked time with America, has rolled by like a procession of steamrollers. It is the same game that Moonlight Graham played in 1905. It is a living part of history, like calico dresses, stone crockery, and threshing crews eating at outdoor tables. It continually reminds us of what once was, like an Indian-head penny in a handful of new coins (*SJ*, 212).

Baseball would truly be a sport for all time.

But Kinsella doesn't merely use recognizable baseball lore and conjure up nostalgic thoughts. What distinguishes his baseball fiction is his tendency to invest the sport with distinct religious overtones. If religion is, according to the *Random House Dictionary*, "a set of beliefs concerning the cause, nature, and purpose of the universe," then several of Kinsella's characters view baseball as a religion. Gideon Clarke's father remembers his first baseball game thus: "And then he took me to a real game. We went into Iowa City and watched a commercial league in action, and it was just like I'd discovered the meaning of the universe" (*IBC*, 40). Of the Cubs and all-stars locked in battle, Gideon remarks, "Baseball is the only thing on the minds of these men. Those who marched to the Crusades had less dedication" (*IBC*, 188). Ray Kinsella thinks of his hearing of the mystical voice as "akin to religious conversion" and declares that a "ballpark at night is more like a church than a church" (*SJ*, 64, 135). Toward the end of the story, Salinger assures Ray that visitors to his ball field will "watch the game, and it will be as if they have knelt in front of a faith healer, or dipped themselves in magic waters where a saint once rose like a serpent and cast benedictions to the wind like peach petals" (*SJ*, 212). Salinger's "rapture" in the last chapter is very much a religious transformation, as in the manner of several 1980s "born again" fundamentalist beliefs; he disappears through the outfield door to the reward of the righteous. At one point Ray undercuts the religious connection somewhat by referring to baseball as just a game: "We're not just ordinary people, we're a congregation. Baseball is a ceremony, a ritual, as surely as sacrificing a goat beneath a full moon is a ritual. The only difference is that most of us realize that it *is* a game" (*SJ*, 72). But later in the novel, all the characters accept Eddie Scissons' equation of baseball to the Word, the Logos. Looking "for all the world like an Old Testament prophet on the side of a mountain," Scissons spouts his "evangelical fervor:" I take the word of baseball and begin to talk it. I begin to speak it. The word is baseball. Say it after me . . . Can you imagine walking around with the very word of baseball enshrined inside you? Because the word of salvation is baseball. It gets inside you. Inside me. And the words that I speak are spirit, and *are* baseball" (*SJ*, 191-2).

Often to reinforce his point about baseball being a true religion, Kinsella ridicules more conventional pieties. In *Shoeless Joe*, he uses satire on Ray's mother-in-law, who has named her four sons after the four gospel writers: "When there were lulls in the conversation she read her Bible, sneering a little in her perfection" (*SJ*, 23). He also mocks Ray's mother gently: "She lives with her sister, my maiden aunt, in a high-rise in Great Falls, Montana, with a cat and a Bible" (*SJ*, 25). As Eddie Scissons rants through his sermon, Ray whispers to Annie, "Your mother should be here" (*SJ*, 192). In a story called "Driving Toward the Moons" from *The Thrill of the Grass*, Kinsella caricatures an elderly landlord couple's decor: "On the dark end-table in the hall is a bland-coloured crocheted doily, its shape recognizable as the face of Jesus. A small shelf in the living room holds religious and inspirational pamphlets and books about Lawrence Welk and his pious entourage. There is a garish, ten-foot *Last Supper* above a fireplace that burns an electric log" (*TG*, 111-2). The same house's "wallpaper in the dining room has about 10,000 pictures of Jesus' head with a green halo around it" (*TG*, 117). This is not to say that Kinsella doesn't appreciate Biblical religion. Indeed, he models much of the story of *The Iowa Baseball Confederacy* on the Old Testament tales of the Deluge, of Gideon and his trumpet, Saul on the road to Damascus, and the Apocalypse. But, for Kinsella, these stories are cause for wild, momentous connections with baseball, not only the smug satisfactions of conventional Bible-toters. He would replace the Jesus-face doilies and wallpaper with shrines to baseball:

> I advocate the establishment of shrines in recognition of baseball greats: Ty Cobb, Tris Speaker, Shoeless Joe Jackson, Ruth, Gehrig, Mantle, Mays, DiMaggio, and a few dozen others. Not just at Cooperstown, but at roadside shrines like the cairns that commemorate cavalry battles, treaty signings, and Indian uprisings. Sites where bleary-eyed travelers could rest for a moment, drink clear water, fill their radiators on broiling afternoons, and study the highlights of their heroes' careers, recorded in bronze and granite (*SJ*, 30).

Could any modern pilgrims ask for more? Kinsella asks rhetorically.

Apparently Phil Alden Robinson, the writer and director of *Field of Dreams*, thought so, and his movie version of *Shoeless Joe* takes the religious theme even farther. *Field of Dreams* trims away Eddie Scissons and Ray's twin brother from the novel, substitutes a black former writer for Salinger, and commits the egregious mistake of having Shoeless Joe bat right-handed and throw left-handed. But the film captures the basic tone of the book and improves on it by fleshing out the meeting of Ray and his father, adding interaction and humor between the ghost-players and Ray, and by giving stunning visual referents for the religious themes. Although it garnered Oscar nominations, including one for best picture, *Field of Dreams* has provoked contrary estimates among critics and viewers. As *Newsweek's* reviewer wrote, "This is the sort of movie you either swallow whole or not at all."[5] Pauline Kael, in *The New Yorker*, dismissed it as "a kinder, gentler crock," as "doggerel emotion, these corn-fed epiphanies."[6] Roger Angell, in the same magazine, complained about "why it's so hard to look at the pastime with a clear gaze." Instead, he lamented, "We seem to want to go on sweetening it up, frosting the flakes, because we want it to say things about ourselves that probably aren't true."[7] *The Nation's* reviewer thought the film "gives wish-fulfillment a bad name."[8] *Time's* Richard Corliss considered it a "male weepie at its wussiest," and though Ron Rosenbaum in *Mademoiselle* gave it a positive review, he, too, joked about the prevalence of Sudden Head Cold Syndrome among male viewers.[9] And some critics chastised Robinson for including a black writer, but having him watch and gush over an all-white fantasy with no Negro League stars on the field.[10]

But even while criticizing *Field of Dreams*, several critics acknowledged its religious bases. Harlan Jacobson, in "Born Again Baseball" in *Film Comment*, decried the film as too Capra-esque but analyzed the last scene, wherein hundreds of cars approach the lit-up field at night, as reflective of deeper dreams:

> What is driving them there? What drove the masses to the mountain in *Close Encounters of the Third Kind* a decade ago—the romance with the mythical future, the alien, the Mother Ship brought to us by our technology—now draws Lost America to its mythical past, the homestead, the dad with the ball and bat. Who can help

> but be touched? We meet ourselves in the past to take a spiritual shower with the boys: *Field of Dreams* is for the fundamentalist batboy inside us.

Jacobson saw Shoeless Joe as supposedly representing the Second Coming, the Son of God.[11] *Vogue's* reviewer quoted Robinson that Jackson was a "symbol of unfulfilled dreams and infinite possibility."[12] David Denby, in *New York,* wondered what Robinson wanted the audience to believe in: "In baseball as America, baseball as the past, baseball implacably forging the links of our personal history. If we deny baseball, we deny ourselves."[13] At least three commentators made the connection between *Field of Dreams* and religion even more explicit. Tom O'Brien in *Commonweal* noted, "The real theme of the film isn't baseball, or America, but sunny summer days spent with loved ones at some ideal house, a pathetic but oh-so-human imagination of heaven."[14] Ralph Novak in *People* put it even more bluntly:

> Resurrection. Redemption. Forgiveness. And all of it taking place on a baseball field. Welcome to the First Church of the Hanging Curveball and Game-Ending Double Play.
>
> Ultimately, in fact, this movie is a lot more about religion than it is about baseball.[15]

And one writer, James M. Wall in *The Christian Century,* found the film demonstrating Soren Kierkegaard's three stages of existence: aesthetic, ethical, and religious. Wall cheered it enthusiastically for its hopeful message.[16] But the firmest, most "authentic" praise may have come from Denver Episcopal bishop William Frey, who allegedly exclaimed after viewing the film, "Did I see what I think I saw? Life after death? A seeker on a spiritual quest? Inner healing? Becoming a child to enter the Kingdom? Losing one's life to gain it? Forgiving and accepting forgiveness?" The same article quoted Wheaton College sociologist James A. Mathisen that baseball "with all its symbolism and ritual, is clearly being used to stand for a common American spiritual quest."[17]

The impact of Kinsella's baseball fiction and *Field of Dreams* may not be ephemeral. The owners of the farmland on which the movie crews constructed the baseball diamond have preserved it as a "shrine" of sorts, as visitors have been showing up in droves to see the field, play catch, melt into the outfield corn, and generally revere the site. In fact one owner who had replanted left field with corn responded to fan requests to restore the outfield, which he has done. Visitors have come from all over the United States and several foreign countries, and one couple even got married there. The landowners, perhaps a little puzzled, have vowed to keep the field as is until tourist interest drops off, requesting only donations for the field's upkeep (and, of course, selling T-shirts). They may wait quite a while, for Kinsella and Robinson may have "struck a profoundly resonant chord in the American psyche."[18] Baseball, already rich in its mythic associations, has added a religious appeal. Consciously working in previous folkloristic traditions about baseball, Kinsella has laid on another layer of a new myth, a religious gloss, which Robinson has decked out in luscious color, making Iowa glow like heaven. In these fruitful artistic interchanges, baseball has once again proved its mythopoeic qualities, its capacity to engender emotional allegiance in an American audience hungering for sustaining myths for generations to come. Who knows? We may look up one day and discover that sod has indeed replaced all the artificial turf, that the foul lines do go on forever, and that our own Shoeless Joes are standing on our own fields of dreams. What myths we will web in that future!

NOTES:

[1]All references to Kinsella's works are to the following editions: *Shoeless Joe* (New York; Ballantine paperback, 1982); *The Iowa Baseball Confederacy* (New York; Ballantine paperback, 1986); *The Thrill of the Grass* (New York: Penguin paperback, 1984); and *The Further Adventures of Slugger McBatt* (Boston: Houghton Mifflin paperback, 1988). All page

references appear in the text within parentheses.

[2]Daniel Okrent, review of *Shoeless Joe, New York Times Book Review,* July 25, 1982, 10.

[3]Eliot Asinof, review of *The Iowa Baseball Confederacy, New York Times Book Review,* April 20, 1986, 14.

[4]W. P. Kinsella, quoted in Brooke K. Horvath and William J. Palmer, "Three On: An Interview with David Carkeet, Mark Harris, and W. P. Kinsella," *Modern Fiction Studies,* v. 33 (Spring 1987), 188.

[5]David Ansen, "Baseball Diamonds are Forever," *Newsweek,* April 24, 1989, 72.

[6]Pauline Kael, "Fascination," *The New Yorker,* May 1, 1989, 76-7.

[7]Roger Angell, "No, But I Saw the Game," *The New Yorker,* July 31, 1989, 56.

[8]Stuart Klawans, "Films," *The Nation,* May 15, 1989, 678.

[9]Richard Corliss, "Don't Run: One Hit, One Error," *Time,* April 24, 1989, 78; Ron Rosenbaum, "What is It With Guys and Baseball?," *Mademoiselle,* (July 1989), 66, 68-9.

[10]Tom O'Brien, "Soaps & Dreams," *Commonweal,* May 19, 1989, 303; Klawans, "Films," *The Nation,* May 15, 1989, 678.

[11]Harlan Jacobson, "Born Again Baseball," *Film Comment* (May/June 1989), 78-9.

[12]"Success Stories," *Vogue* (May 1989), 204.

[13]David Denby, "Soft Ball," *New York,* April 24, 1989, 98.

[14]O'Brien, "Soaps & Dreams," *Commonweal,* May 19, 1989, 303.

[15]Ralph Novak, "Picks & Pans," *People,* May 15, 1989, 13.

[16]James M. Wall, "A Playing Field for the Boys of Eternity," *The Christian Century,* May 17, 1989, 515.

[17]Terry Mattingly, "Hit Movie Played on a Religious Field," *Rocky Mountain News,* May 27, 1989, 105.

[18]Rogers Worthington, "*Field of Dreams* Diamond an Iowa Shrine," *The Sunday Denver Post Contemporary,* April 15, 1990, 21, 23; see also Mark Donovan and Margaret Nelson, "For *Field of Dreams* Fans Who Trek to Don Lansing's Iowa Farm, the Diamond is Forever," *People,* October 23, 1989, 120-1.

Half-Cultivated Fields: Symbolic Landscapes of Baseball

By DAVE HEALY and PAUL HEALY

IN DISCUSSIONS OF AMERICAN sports it has become commonplace to make observations about how various games treat time. Baseball, we are reminded, is potentially timeless, a game divided by units of activity rather than by units of time, while football and basketball, the other two members of Michael Novak's (*The Joy of Sports*) "holy trinity," are governed by the clock. Less is said in these discussions about the variable of space. Novak alludes to it briefly and is surely correct when he says, "Baseball, basketball, and football do not take place just anywhere. There are consecrated places." But though they may have in common a sacred quality, the landscapes of our sports, the playing fields and courts, are more notable for their differences—differences which have much to say about the symbolic representations of the American dream in the games Americans play. And when these differences are subjected to careful scrutiny, the baseball field emerges as the richest and most complex symbol of the American experience.

Historian Perry Miller has described the American experiment as an "errand into the wilderness." One of the imperatives of that errand was to render the wilderness tame, to subdue Nature, to explore, conquer, domesticate, and cultivate—to build what John Winthrop called "a city upon a hill" which all the world could observe. Insofar as conquering the wilderness was concerned, the American errand was strikingly successful. The virgin land became a garden—a field and a park and a city. However, once the transition from unbounded to bounded space was complete and the frontier closed, the nature of the American errand changed. Americans still thought of themselves as pioneers, but now, with the physical frontier gone, they needed to find symbolic ways of fulfilling their destiny. The rise of American sport in the nineteenth century may be seen as one such symbolic expression of the American pioneer spirit, for as Ronald Cummings ("The Superbowl Society") has observed, "Our modern sports are attempts to break out of an artificially imposed confinement." Time and space are the two dimensions of that confinement, and here we are especially interested in exploring the significance of space. The landscapes of American sports represent varying degrees of artificially imposed confinement and varying degrees of accommodation to a conquered wilderness, but it is baseball which most fully and elegantly dramatizes the uniquely American tension between civilization and wildness.

The closest thing to wilderness on a "playing field" occurs at a place one does not ordinarily refer to as a field (the very term "field" suggests some degree of taming). It is on the golf course where an errant shot is almost always in danger of straying into the "wilderness." It is the fair but narrow way that the resolute golfer is to walk in, shunning the rough, the sand, the water—all the uncultivated natural elements.

But in most of our games, certainly among the "holy trinity," the wilderness has—except for symbolic representations—disappeared. Indeed, America's only truly indigenous game, basketball, which Pete Axthelm rightly calls "the city game," was created indoors to meet the needs of a populace quite cut off from the wilderness. Basketball is the only member of the "holy trinity" that was truly invented; the other games evolved—football from rugby, baseball from rounders and cricket. And because it was invented in the city for city dwellers, basketball is the furthest removed from Nature. Played on a court rather than a field, it has forsaken its peach-basket goals for forged iron bolted to fiberglass. Its space is carefully circumscribed and divided into zones which may be occupied for only limited amounts of time by ten oversized bodies which are obliged to live and move and have their being in an area not much bigger than some suburban family rooms.

Only slightly less removed from the wilderness is the football field, whose very name, the gridiron, evokes an image of Jeffersonian yeoman farms, each laid out in symmetrical squares that turn the entire landscape into a huge sheet of graph paper. Some natural or "wild" elements remain—e.g., the pigskin, sometimes called the "seed"—but like basketball, football depends upon keeping the ball "in play" and demands complete accommodation to the confines of bounded space.

Baseball is the only game played in a park, a term which embodies the tension that baseball so carefully maintains, a tension between the competing claims of civilization and wilderness. The baseball field is carefully cultivated and bounded, but it opens up from a point produced by the convergence of two perpendicular lines to a potentially limitless expanse for which the outfield fence serves as only the most artificial and arbitrary of barriers, just as the elusive "frontier" served for the original pioneers. In the older ball parks, the symbolic nature of the outfield wall was sometimes heightened by letting vines grow over it, while in other parks the limit of the frontier was marked by that most American of civilization's expressions: the advertisement.

The tension between civilization and wilderness on the baseball field grows out of the contrast between the infield and outfield. The former is rigorously standardized, the distance from the outside of first base to the outside of third base and from the back of home plate to the middle of second base being specified as 127 feet, 3 and 3/8 inches. Like the diamond after which it is named, the infield is a natural object that has been subjected to the most careful and regularized human fabrication. The outfield, on the other hand, is expansive and idiosyncratic, especially in the older ball parks. The old Polo Grounds, home of the New York Giants from 1911-1957 and the Mets from 1962-1963, was a monument to idiosyncrasy: 279 feet to left, 483 to center, and 257 to right. So spacious were the power alleys that the bullpens were located in fair territory. Or consider the former home of the Pirates, Forbes Field (1909-1970).

In 62 seasons, no one ever pitched a no-hitter there, which may have had something to do with the park's odd dimensions: 365 feet to left, 457 to center, and 300 to right. And then there was Braves Field, finally scaled down to 340-390-320 dimensions from the original design of 402 feet down the lines and 505 to center.

The inhabitants of these two realms, infield and outfield, may be created equal, but they have different mythic roles and differing status in the popular imagination. It is significant, for example, that the outfielder, specifically the center fielder, is most likely to achieve mythic status. Honus Wagner, Brooks Robinson, Rogers Hornsby—the game's greats who labored in the infield have never achieved quite the heroic stature of the great center fielders: Mantle, Mays, DiMaggio. These latter heroes are more easily romanticized, in part because of the greater space they tended. Daniel Boone, the representative frontiersman, is said to have so cherished "elbow room" that he pulled up stakes and moved whenever anyone settled within a hundred miles of him. The outfielder is a latter-day frontiersman whose freedom is closely tied to the amount of vacant space around him. The infielder, on the other hand, is an heir of the yeoman farmer, a tiller of the soil who carefully grooms his small plot of plowed land and guards it against incursions by enemy forces.

The baseball field puts one in mind of Leo Marx's (*The Machine in the Garden*) conception of the pastoral genre in literature: a mode of reconciliation that seeks out and presents a middle landscape between the city and the forest. One is also reminded of the American pastoralist Thoreau and his depiction of his bean field near Walden Pond: "Mine was, as it were, the connecting link between wild and cultivated fields, as some states are civilized, and others half-civilized, and others savage or barbarous, so my field was, though not in a bad sense, a half-cultivated field."

It is within the confines of a half-cultivated field that our latter-day pioneer, the baseball player, must make his endless journey. The implements of his craft look backward to a confrontation starkly primitive: after affirming his attachment to the land by rubbing his hands with dirt, he grabs his hewn stick of ash and attacks the hellish horsehide hurled hideously at his head. If he meets the challenge successfully, the imagery becomes abruptly modern as he turns the spheroid into a temporary satellite screaming over the earth below. Then he is ready to leave home and, like his pilgrim forebears, establish outposts of civilization where he can be safe. Or, in the ultimate achievement, he sends his satellite beyond the known world, transcending the frontier and rendering the wilderness benign as he trots home in his own good time.

Historian David Noble (*The American Adam*) has represented the American dream as a drama of leaving home. The first home to be left was Europe, but once here Americans continued to leave home for the ever-advancing frontier. Huck Finn is our representative hero in this regard, lighting out for the territory in order to flee the corrupting influences of civilization. Today our pinstripe-clad Hucks re-enact the archetypal journey with each trip to the plate. Their object is to leave home, then, like Odysseus, successfully navigate their way through hostile territory, and finally return as conquering heroes. The baseball player thus ultimately breaks ranks with the prototypical American literary hero, for the ball player has learned that you *can* go home again. Having arrived, though, he knows that he must leave again, destined to continually re-enact the drama of the American pilgrimage.

We have suggested that the baseball field represents a "middle landscape" between civilization and wilderness, and that this landscape results in large part from the tension between the bounded, cultivated, regimented, "civilized" infield; and the expansive, idiosyncratic wilderness of the outfield. Other features of baseball's landscape reinforce and enrich this fundamental tension.

Consider the "dugout," for example. In other sports the area where players sit when they are not on the field is called the "bench." Its occupants sit in full view of the spectators and the opposing team. But baseball players descend into and emerge from a dugout, again revealing a kinship with their pioneer ancestors, who hacked their first crude dwelling places out of the sod. The dugout, then, is a place of refuge, of hiding, of escape from the howling wilderness.

The old-fashioned "bullpen" was another such refuge, a place of privacy, a kind of world-within-a-world outpost of civilization, a fort from which the harried wagon master could summon relief to douse the flames of enemy arrows. The "pitcher's mound" is perhaps baseball's most complex geographical symbol. Circular in shape, like the American Indian tepee, it occupies the very center of civilization—as did the ziggurats and other sacred shrines of ancient societies. Its sacred quality is further enhanced by its elevation. Indeed, it is almost impossible to miss the connection between pitcher's mound and burial mound. Seen in this light, the mound becomes a symbol of the final frontier—death—and the pitcher becomes our greatest hero, for it is he who dances on the grave.

If, as Cummings claims, sports represent an artificially imposed confinement which must be transcended, then baseball is distinctive in its treatment of confines, of boundaries. At first glance, the world of the infield and its surroundings seems almost excessively bounded. The would-be hitter emerges from the dugout to occupy the on-deck circle. From there he moves to the batter's box, a four feet by six feet prison outside of which he must not stray. If he is fortunate enough to flee this confinement by hitting the ball, he is greeted by another boundary—the base path, that straight and narrow way which is found by few. His actions on these paths are guided by the first and third-base coaches, who are themselves confined to their respective coaching boxes. The civilized world seems a place of rigid confinement.

However, when one observes the way the game is actually played, one discovers an abundance of fluidity and accommodation. The on-deck circle turns out to be mostly an ornament; few on-deck hitters actually perch there. The batter's box has by the second or third inning lost most of its definition, and its boundaries are subject to interpretation—an interpretation that certain hitters (one thinks of Tony Oliva) are inclined to press to the limit. And what of the base path? It, too, proves to be an imaginary rather than a real limit, for the literal line is routinely transgressed by sliding runners attempting to take out the second baseman, as well as by anyone rounding third and heading for home. First and third-base coaches are often found outside their coaching boxes. Pitchers, who are supposed to maintain contact with the rubber until the ball is released, in fact need only keep their push-off foot near it. Second basemen and shortstops, for their part, though they are supposed to be on second when making a force out, actually have some latitude—as do the base runners who attempt to thwart their efforts. The strike, which supposedly is only as fluid as an individual batter's dimensions, in point of fact differs from umpire to umpire, from league to league, and from pitch to pitch (witness "the old automatic" on 3 and 0).

What is one to make of these fluid boundaries? What is the point of defining space so rigidly but then relaxing those definitions through interpretation and accommodation? The observer who is unable to see and appreciate the symbolic nature of baseball's geography will be hard pressed to answer such questions. If, however, one is attuned to the symbolism of baseball's geographical landscapes, it is not difficult to take the next logical step and to begin making connections between the geographical and the anthropological or psychological or spiritual.

Thus far we have suggested that the geography of the baseball field has much to say about the American experience with Nature. It seems clear that the ball park is a place to learn about human nature as well. Just as baseball's definition of space serves to dramatize the tension between civilization and wildness in the American experience, so too does baseball's fluid interpretation of its rigidly defined physical boundaries dramatize a spiritual tension in the very nature of man—a tension between legalism on the one hand, and antinomianism on the other.

Our forebears were pioneers of the physical frontier, and as their heirs, we must find symbolic ways to express our pioneer spirit; baseball, it has been suggested here, is one such symbolic expression. Spiritually, our Puritan forebears tended toward religious dogmatism and extremism. For the Puritan, the boundaries of the batter's box or baseline would have been clear and absolute; any deviation would have been severely punished. But while it is easy for moderns to lampoon the Puritans' rigidity, we are likely to admit, in our more balanced and reflective moments, that human intercourse does require some boundaries, some rules of conduct. Antinomianism has never been accepted by the vast majority of Americans in any generation.

Baseball, then, proves to be an ideal model, not only of the complex relationship of human beings to Nature, but also of the complex realities of human nature itself. Baseball's landscapes are not only geographical; they also have a psychological and a symbolic dimension. On the one hand, their rigid definition is a tribute to the human need for order, limits, specificity, and clarity. On the other hand, the way in which those definitions are interpreted in practice is a tribute to the human need for self-expression, for good old-fashioned Yankee ingenuity, as it were.

The double play captures this tension as succinctly as anything does. The runner bearing down on second is the prototypical American pioneer. He has ventured away from the safety of home and then the fort (first base). Yet his path is circumscribed: He must stay in the baseline. (No anarchist he, the decision about which direction to proceed around the bases is not a decision at all.) But just where is the baseline? Ay, there's the rub. And it is within the latitude afforded by that rub that human inventiveness flourishes. Furthermore, baseball, being scrupulously fair, provides a corresponding latitude to the baserunner's defensive counterpart, for whom the definition of second base and his possession of the ball while occupying it is also a matter of interpretation.

The American dream has always been complex, even contradictory. At the heart of the dream's ambivalence is the dichotomy between wilderness and civilization and the American attempt to experience the best of both worlds. "I wish," wrote Emerson in 1844, "to have rural strength and religion for my children. . . and I wish city facility and polish. I find with chagrin that I cannot have both." Nearly a century and a half later, many Americans still identify with Emerson's lament. But even if we, like him, discover that we cannot have both, we can symbolically experience the best of both worlds in that most American and human and humane of environments—the ball park.

Diamond Stars: Baseball Astrology

By JOHN B. HOLWAY

JIMINY CHRISTMAS! By the great heavenly stars! Was Rickey Henderson *born* to steal bases?

You bet your sweet ephemeris he was.

Henderson was born Christmas Day, 1958, a good day to be born if you want to grow up to be a big league base-stealing champion. For that makes him a Capricorn (December 22-January 19). In fact, he was born almost exactly 99 years after Hugh Nicol, the flying Scot, who set the old record (that still stands) of 138 back in 1887. Nicol was born New Year's Day 1858. Another Capricorn speedster, Max Carey (born January 11, 1890), led the league in steals 10 times.

Since 1876, 197 big league stolen base crowns have been won, and Capricorns have captured 29 of them, well above their fair share of 16.

But look at Pisces (February 19-March 20) like Bert Campaneris: They've won 31, twice as many as they should be expected to win.

Down at the other end of the list, the poor Cancers (June 20-July 22) have won only three of the 197 titles. Latest to do it was Willie Wilson in 1979. Now there's a man who seems to have figuratively outrun his stars.

What are the chances of such a distribution—31 on the high side, three on the low—occurring by chance? To find out, I asked Pete Palmer, statistician and co-author of *The Hidden Game of Baseball*. Pete punched some numbers into his computer and came up with the answer. This could indeed have happened by chance—once in 10 million times.

Note that the top six signs account for 75 percent of all stolen-base titles, the bottom six only 25 percent.

Note also that winter babies (Pisces, Capricorn, Aquarius) account for 71 titles, summer babies only 26, or about one-third as many.

Palmer questions whether repeat winners should be allowed, saying they skew the averages unfairly. Personally, I feel that a Luis Aparicio, with nine titles, deserves more weight than a Topsy Hartsel, with one. So we decided to do it both ways—total championships and total individual champions—and let the reader take his choice.

Pisces leads the total titles list with 16 percent. It also leads the total individual champions list with 14.5 percent. However, since the second list is less than half as large, the odds go down dramatically. It is far harder to toss 90 heads out of 100 than to toss nine heads out of 10. The percentages are the same, but the odds are vastly different.

Anyway, the odds on individual winners came to 40-1. Statisticians say anything over 20-1 is "significant." So, using even conservative numbers, the data pretty well rule out chance as an explanation.

Base-Stealing Champions

Sign	*Date*		*Titles*
Pisces	Feb 19-Mar 20	31	Companeris 6, Wagner 5, Reiser 2, Ashburn
Capricorn	Dec 22-Jan 19	29	Carey 10, Henderson 7, Taveras, Nicol
Sagittarius	Nov 22-Dec 21	25	Cobb 6, Minoso 3, Bruton 3, Moreno 2
Taurus	Apr 20-May 20	24	Aparicio 9, Mays 4, Lopes 2, North 2, Otis
Gemini	May 21-June 20	19	Brock 8, Werber 3, Galan 2, LeFlore 2
Virgo	Aug 23-Sept 22	21	Raines 4, Cuyler 4, Dillinger 3, Frisch 3, Coleman 3
Libra	Sept 23-Oct 22	13	Wills 6, Patek, Murtaugh, Crosetti
Aquarius	Jan 20-Feb 18	11	J Robinson 2, Schoendienst
Scorpio	Oct 23-Nov 21	11	Case 6, Stirnweiss 2, Rivers, Tolan
Aries	Mar 21-Apr 19	6	Sisler 4, Milan 2
Leo	Jul 23-Aug 22	4	Reese, Frey, Isbel
Cancer	Jun 21-Jul 22	3	W Wilson, Rivera, Hartsel
	Total:	*197*	

Numbers like these intrigue me. A stubborn Scorpio, I began checking data in a dozen categories—presidents, congressmen, Academy Award winners, Nobel laureates, Pulitzer Prize winners, and on and on.

Of course I was especially anxious to check the old wives' tale that Scorpios make the best lovers and wrote to Masters and Johnson to see if they had any data on that. They replied huffily that they don't lend themselves to such research. A pity. Science will always be the poorer for it.

Meanwhile, you don't have to believe in astrology to read statistics, and the data I found made me pause and scratch my head and ask "Why?"

I should say that I also did a thorough study of biorhythms and sports, checking over 1,000 performances in baseball, football, tennis, track and field, boxing, and swimming. I found absolutely no statistical confirmation of this seemingly scientific but—I'm convinced—actually fraudulent theory. If anyone wants to bet on the World Series, the Super Bowl, or a heavyweight title fight on the basis of biorhythm alone, let him see me. I'll be glad to take his money.

On the other hand, astrology, which smacks of unscientific magic, produces numbers far outside what the law of averages says is normal. It seems downright unfair that a man's birthday can give him an advantage in stealing bases or hitting home runs, but then life has always been unfair. Athletes are not typical of the rest of us. They're taller, heavier, have better eyesight, better muscle tone, superior hand-eye coordination, and so on. They also differ, I now must add, in their birthdays.

Big League Stars

Palmer was also skeptical, so like a good SABR (Society for American Baseball Research) member, he decided to do some scientific checking. He ran a massive computer study on all 9,388 men who had played major league baseball from 1909 through

1981. His read-out produced an almost perfect sine curve of births arranged along the calendar year.

If you want to grow up to be a big league player, Palmer found, you'd be wise to plan to be born roughly between July 20 and Christmas, that is, from Leo through Sagittarius. The best time of all is late summer. Virgo (August 24-September 23) has produced 921 players, or 18 percent more than normal. Virgo leads at every position except shortstop and third base.

The worst time to be born is early spring, as an Aries (March 21 to April 20). Only 681 big league players were born then, 11 percent below normal, and 35 percent less than those born Virgos. This is almost the same result I got in a study of pro football players in 1977. Virgo was way out in front, Aries next to last.

Suppose you throw 9,388 darts at a large round dart board divided into 12 slices and spinning furiously. Assuming that all the darts hit the board, what is the chance that 921 will land in one section and only 681 in another?

The chance, Palmer found, is more than 700 million to one!

Of course not all slices of the zodiacal pie are exactly the same size. Cancer has 32 days, Pisces 29. And births are not distributed equally throughout the calendar. However, authorities disagree on which are the high-birth months and which the low. One study says Gemini (May 22-June 21) has the least births, Aquarius (January 21-February 19) the most. But another study is just the other way around.

At any rate, the difference is not great, 15 percent at most. It hardly explains why Pisces has more than 10 times as many stolen base championships as Cancer.

But, strangely, Palmer found, although Virgos get on the team more than anyone else, once they're in uniform they don't particularly excel. They're about average in combined batting average and home runs among hitters, as well as ERA and won-lost records for pitchers.

About the only outstanding Virgos in big league annals are Ted Williams, Roger Maris, Frank Robinson, and Larry Lajoie. Virgos are supposed to be painstaking perfectionists. If that's true, it certainly describes Williams at least. And if there is any validity to these data, then Ted, who had to overcome so much—five years at war, a difficult home park, a variety of injuries—apparently had to overcome his stars as well.

Batting Champs

Palmer's study reveals another anomaly. Aries, the least likely to get on a team, are collectively the best hitters once they do land a job. Their combined batting average is .267. The average for all signs if .262. Leo (mid-summer) has the worst average, .259.

The batting average curve is almost the exact opposite of the total players' curve, with above average figures in the late winter and early spring (Pisces through Taurus) and average or below average figures for the rest of the year.

My own study of 208 big league batting champs, 1876-1987, confirms Palmer's findings: Two spring signs, Aries and Taurus, are among the tops in producing batting champions. Late winter and early spring are the high periods. All other signs, except Sagittarius, are average or below.

If Scorpio Stan Musial had been born one day later, his seven titles would have put Sagittarius out of reach—for the present, at least.

Stan is not the only champ to overcome his stars. The 1985 king, Willie McGee, is also a Scorpio. Wade Boggs has won four titles so far for the next-to-last Geminis. And Bill Madlock won four for last-place Capricorn, which proves, perhaps—as the astrologers admit—that the stars impel, they don't compel. Long shots do come in. I just wouldn't bet on them, that's all.

(Chart next page)

Batting Champions

Sign	*Titles*	
Taurus	28	Hornsby 7, Brett 2, Mattingly, Gwynn 2, Mays
Sagittarius	25	Cobb 12, DiMaggio 2, Buckner, Kaline, Kuenn, Garr
Aries	23	Rose 3, Waner 3, Sisler 2, Appling 2, Speaker
Pisces	21	Wagner 8, Ashburn 2, Reiser
Libra	17	Carew 7, Foxx 2, Oliver, Hernandez, Mantle
Leo	15	Clemente 4, Heilmann 4, Yastrzemski 3
Cancer	15	Oliva 3, W Wilson, Torre, Boudreau
Virgo	15	T Williams 6, Lajoie 3, F Robinson, Carty, Raines
Aquarius	14	Aaron 2, Lansford, Lynn, Ruth, J Robinson
Scorpio	13	Musial 7, McGee, Terry
Gemini	14	Boggs 4, Simmons 2, B Williams, Gehrig
Capricorn	9	Madlock 4, M Alou, Mize
Total:	*209*	

Let's look at the favorites. Taurus, Sagittarius, and Aries make up 25 percent of the zodiac but account for 36 percent of all batting championships, over half of all .400 hitters, and more than half of the lifetime 3,000-hit men. Two of the three, Sagittarius and Aries, have produced the six longest batting streaks of this century—Sagittarians Cobb (twice) and DiMaggio, and Aries Rose, Sisler, and Holmes.

The quintessential baseball Aries is Pete Rose. Who can forget the image of Rose barreling into catcher Ray Fosse to win the 1974 All Star game, a scene as indelibly engraved into the baseball psyche as the famous photo of Cobb flying into third with spikes flashing?

Aries are the "I am," take-charge egotists of the zodiac; they supposedly love the spotlight and usually hog it in conversation and everything else. Aries lead all other signs in winning Academy Awards (Marlon Brando, Gregory Peck, Paul Newman, Spencer Tracy, William Holden, Bette Davis, Joan Crawford, Liza Minelli).

Capricorns come next to Sagittarius in the calendar, but they rank at the bottom among batting champions, with only nine. One of those was Elmer Flick, who won in 1906 with a .306 average, second lowest winning average ever.

Home Runs

Home run champions show a strong preference for being born in the autumn and winter. All of these signs, except Capricorn, are average or above. All the spring and summer signs, without exception, are average and below.

The best sign of all for power hitters is Libra. Out of 220 home run titles won or shared since 1876, Libras have won 34, five times as many as last-place Gemini. Libra Mike Schmidt alone has won eight crowns. Mickey Mantle, Jimmie Foxx, and Chuck Klein each won four, and Ed Mathews two.

Thanks to Schmidt, Libra has now vaulted into first place, overtaking the mighty Aquarians—Babe Ruth, Hank Aaron, Ernie Banks, and Ben Oglivie—who had been kings of the sluggers until Schmidt brought the Age of Aquarius to an end.

Darrell Evans is another one who overcame the accident of birth. He's not only the oldest home run champ, he's a Gemini, the least likely sign to lead the league.

The greatest slugger of all, Negro Leaguer Josh Gibson, was a Sagittarius. Sadaharu Oh of Japan is a Taurus.

Home Run Champions

Sign	*Titles*	
Libra	35	Schmidt 8, Mantle 4, Foxx 4, Klein 4, Matthews 2, McGwire
Aquarius	28	Ruth 12, Aaron 4, Banks 2, Oglivie
Pisces	28	Ott 6, Rice 3, Murphy 2, Stargell 2, Allen 2, Baker 2, Murray
Sagittarius	27	Kingman 3, Foster 2, DiMaggio 2, Thomas, Bench
Taurus	18	Jackson 4, Mays 4, H Wilson 4, Hornsby 2
Scorpio	18	Kiner 7, Dw Evans, Sievers
Cancer	18	Killebrew 6, Armas, Dawson
Virgo	15	T Williams 4, Maris, F Robinson, Cepeda, Snider
Aries	14	Cravath 6
Capricorn	13	Mize 4, Greenberg 4, McCovey 3, Conigliaro, Grich
Leo	8	Howard 2, Nettles, Yastrzemski, Colavito
Gemini	6	Gehrig 3, Da Evans
Total:	*228*	

As the chart shows, autumn through winter (Libra through Pisces) is the best time to be born if you want to grow up to be a home run champ. But the month-to-month swings are too erratic to sustain any simple seasonal theory. Aquarius, with 28 home run titles, for example, comes right after Capricorn, with only 13. There is obviously something else at work here besides the earth's journey around the sun. If it is not astrology, whatever it may be deserves some serious study.

April 8, 1974 was a particularly good day for Aquarians. If Hank Aaron had let his eye stray from the sports pages for a moment, he would have read in Sydney Omarr's syndicated horoscope column the following forecast for himself.

Advancement indicated. Views are vindicated. You receive compliments from professional superior. You make significant gains. Profit potential increases. . . . Standing in the community is elevated.

That night Hank Aaron went out and hit his million-dollar 715th home run, the one that broke Babe Ruth's record.

Pitchers—ERA

Pitchers show a different profile altogether.

Palmer found that there have been more Virgo pitchers in the big leagues than any other sign, just as there are more Virgos in general. Capricorn has produced the fewest pitchers.

Yet, Virgos are only average as a group once they get on the team. Sagittarians, like Steve Carlton, have the best combined won-lost record, as well as the best combined earned run average. Cancers have the worst won-lost mark, Geminis the worst ERA.

My own study of ERA champs shows that Steve McCatty and JR Richard have pitched their sign into first place among individual winners, edging Aries (Don Sutton, Phil Niekro, Cy Young) by 28 to 27. The two signs incidentally come next to each other on the calendar—late winter and early spring.

Yet, again, the month-to-month differences are so large they rule out an easy seasonal explanation. Aquarius comes right before Pisces on the calendar, but it's dead last in ERA titles, with only seven.

ERA Champions

Sign	*Titles*	
Pisces	28	Grove 9, Alexander 5, McCatty, Richard
Aries	27	Joss 2, Young, Sutton, P Niekro, Hunter
Libra	21	Palmer 2, Capra, McCormick, Podres, Waddell, Scott
Scorpio	20	Johnson 5, Seaver 3, Gooden, Rogers, Candelaria, Gibson, Marichal
Cancer	19	Hubbell 3, Covaleskie 2, Stieb, Pena, Sutcliffe, Tanana, Lopat
Leo	19	Mathewson 5, Wilhelm 2, Blue, Fidrych, Clemens
Capricorn	16	Koufax 5, R Jones, Wynn, Lyons
Virgo	14	Guidry 2, Chandler 2, McDowell, Hoyt
Taurus	13	Spahn 3, Peters 2, Newhouser 2, Walsh 2, Key
Sagittarius	12	Tiant 2, Gomez 2, Carlton, Swan, Burdette
Gemini	9	Chance, Parnell, Cicotte
Aquarius	9	Ryan 2, Hammaker, Bosman, Reynolds, Ruth
Total:	*207*	

Aquarian Nolan Ryan was really bucking the stars when he won in 1981. However, Aquarians are the only sign to produce one man who won all three titles—ERA, home runs, and batting. His name of course was Babe Ruth. (But note that Babe gave up pitching and took up slugging full time. Did his stars impel him?)

For four straight years, 1982-1985, Cancer produced one of the two ERA kings—Rich Honeycutt, Alejandro Pena, Rick Sutcliffe, and Dave Stieb.

Pitchers—Strikeouts

Power hitters differ astrologically from single hitters. Do power pitchers, the strikeout kings, also differ from finesse pitchers, the ERA champs?

They sure do.

I haven't counted all the individual strikeout titles won, but on the list of the ten top strikeout pitchers of all time, four are Scorpios—Walter Johnson, Tom Seaver, Bob Gibson and Jim Bunning. A fifth Scorpio, Bob Feller, would surely be on the list, perhaps at the top of it, if he hadn't lost his four best years in the Navy. Two Scorpio youngsters will probably join the list within fifteen years—Dwight Gooden and Fernando Valenzuela.

Nolan Ryan, the all-time champ, is an Aquarius, the only one in the top ten. The entire list, as of Opening Day 1987, is included in this chart.

All-Time Strikeout Leaders Through 1986

Pitcher	*Sign*	*SO*
Nolan Ryan	Aquarius	4547
Steve Carlton	Sagittarius	4131
Tom Seaver	Scorpio	3640
Gaylord Perry	Virgo	3534
Don Sutton	Aries	3530
Walter Johnson	Scorpio	3508
Phil Niekro	Aries	3342
Ferguson Jenkins	Sagittarius	3192
Bob Gibson	Scorpio	3117
Jim Bunning	Scorpio	2855

(The leading strikeout pitcher until 1987, with 4490—Japan's Masaichi Kaneda—is a Leo.)

Will the day ever come when big league scouts will carry a book of horoscopes along with a stop watch and the other tools of their trade?

Charlie O. Finley, boss of the Oakland A's, dabbled in astrology, though perhaps he was more interested in the astrologer, a beautiful redhead named Laurie Brady, than in astrology. At any rate, Brady predicted in 1970 that the A's would win the division crown in '71 and then the World Series three years in a row. They did. In '76 Finley asked her to do daily charts on every player on the roster.

Manager Chuck Tanner promptly threw them in the waste basket. Perhaps he should have read them: That year the A's failed to win the division for the first time in six seasons.

Only one player has ever admitted to using astrology: Wes Ferrell, who won 20 games six different times for the Red Sox and Indians in the 1930s. An Aquarius, Ferrell "freely admits that his fortunes are governed by the stars," *Washington Post* columnist Shirley Povich wrote in July 1938. "Astrology rules his life. He is a confirmed disciple and credits astrology with curing the soreness in his arm when all other methods failed, including the ministration of medical and bone specialists, quacks and voodoo doctors."

Povich continued: "On the days the stars say they are in his favor he will be the picture of confidence on the pitching mound. He says that several years ago when he was with Cleveland he had his horoscope read and a re-check of his season's victories revealed that he had won ball games on days when the stars were favorable and had lost games when, according to the horoscope, the days were due to be 'bad.'

"He makes no bones about his faith in astrology. He points out that it was more than a coincidence two years ago at Griffith Stadium when, on the same day, Joe Cronin was beaned and Rick Ferrell suffered a broken finger. 'It was a bad day for people born in the sign of Libra,' said Wes, 'and the chart showed it. Both Cronin and Rick were Libra babies.'"

Did it work? Well, Ferrell won 193 big league games, including 25 in 1935 to lead the league.

Reading List

If astrology can predict the future, it should be able to "predict" the past. I went to two astrologers—Laurie Brady of Salem, Massachusetts, and Maude Chalfant of Washington, D.C.—and gave them the birthdays of several athletes and asked them to describe the men, knowing nothing else about them. Then I asked them to tell what might have happened to each on a particular day in his career. Their readings follow. See if you can guess who the players were.

I. Born: February 6, 1895: A very emotional chart. He either had an explosive temper or explosive energy, so if he were a baseball player, I would think he was one of your home run hitters, or a heavyweight boxer.

He had sort of a tormented life, lots of problems. There were definitely problems in his natal home. His father or mother sat on him real hard. There was probably quarreling in the home, or a separation or divorce or loss of parent. He was extremely independent and hard to manage.

There's a very heavy emphasis in the House of Show Business, and Sports in general. He probably loved kids, and I would imagine he had many love affairs.

EVENT: October 1, 1932: I'm wondering, was this person having some health problems? It could be a chart where a person was retiring, or the end of his career was coming. It could have been home runs if this was a baseball player.

II. Born: August 30, 1918: He is terribly independent, probably was very hard to manage. He might have been frustrated, had to control himself, or was made to control himself. He has a fiery way of thinking, and fire in his hands. Anything to do with the hands would be good for him. I'm sure he had emotional problems, probably drinking problems, although I could be very wrong. There's a strong emphasis on his House of Self-Undoing.

He's precise, a Virgo, very exacting in details about everything. He has a quick mind, but he might have been sarcastic in his speech. He could have acted like a dictator to his friends. This is a psychic person, I'm sure, very sensitive.

III. Born: October 25, 1923: A terribly intense person, fixed and stubborn, but very sweet-natured, likeable, and very lucky. He might be a quarterback if he's in football. He would be a power hitter if he's in baseball.

EVENT: October 5, 1951: I think this event was a very happy one. The moon was touching Venus, meaning that sweet things were coming to him or being stirred up. Jupiter in his House of

Work also means good things. Uranus, the planet of Change and Surprise, was exactly over his Pluto (energy). So, whatever this was, it was probably unexpected and very strong and explosive. And very fateful. It's kind of hard to read whether it was pure luck or whether it wasn't.

IV. Born: April 14, 1941: This is a strong, strong person. Super strong. A lot of self-confidence. He was born with it. Even before he opened his eyes, he knew what he wanted.

He's aggressive. He was born with that too. And stubborn. He wanted what he wanted when he wanted it. He rushes into things, just shoots out and does what he thinks he has to do.

When he's playing, he's totally into it. His whole being—his brain, his body—are all working for one thing.

He's got tons of physical energy. His friends would think he's courageous. His enemies would consider him pushy.

Sometimes he can be very strong-willed, rebellious, anti-social, when Mars hits him. All of a sudden he can turn into a really raging person. These are tendencies from birth; he may have mellowed since then. If his energy were all kept inside him, he'd probably hurt people. But he releases it physically in sport.

I would think he's extremely dextrous. His timing is excellent. He moves like a panther. He moves beautifully.

He's got a quick mind, like a hair trigger. Really, really fast mental chemistry. He had sort of a conflict with his relatives. He's quarrelsome and independent. He was kind of noisy as a child, or could have been.

He would also have to learn the value of sexuality. I think when he was younger he would rush into love affairs. But I think he's outgrown that. He's very charming and attractive. He may not be beautiful, but he's bewitching. He has this inner charm. It's more than just charm. I see a little gleam in his eye.

But he's better off when he does things on his own. Any mates would probably be jealous of him. He's dominating, and he attracts people who have a lot of needs, especially females, very sexual, who want a lot and are very demanding. He's sort of restless at home, a high-tension person, lots of nervous energy.

He's creative, though he might put it all into his sport. He's a lot more intellectual than people know.

I think he has a powerful position, because he has such drive, such energy. He needs power. He likes to be on top. If he were in politics, look out!

I like him, whoever he is. I would want to stay away from him with a ten-foot pole, as a female. But I think he's dynamite. He's a real power.

EVENT: August 1, 1978. I get the feeling there has been a lot of strife going on. He may have been very aggressive in the few days just before this. He's so damn strong, you'd think he could overcome almost anything that goes wrong. But he may have been a little disappointed. Things may not have turned out the way he wanted them to.

V. Born May 18, 1946: He's a Taurus, which is a fixed, sort of placid, slow-moving person who is very interested in money. He's very lucky with money. He might be a little erratic with it, but I think he will make good money.

He probably has tremendous energy and heavy hands.

I'm sure he's very charming. Probably women like him. He could be flirtatious and have lots of affairs.

He's really introverted, except for his moon that brings him in front of the public. I think he's ambitious and driving hard for what he wants, and the public pulls him out.

I suspect he's a little hard to handle because of that stubborn Taurus sun: "Don't tell me what to do." He probably loses his temper very easily. He might have a tendency to flare up and speak more angrily than he means to. He's probably impulsive and quarrelsome.

EVENT: October 18, 1977. A terrific massing of planets in his House of Work. The north node of the moon—the lucky part—the moon itself, the sun, Pluto, and Venus—which usually means nice things and gifts—are all in his House of Work. This was just a fantastic day with all those planets—half of all his planets—all in one place. On the whole, I would think this was a fortunate event.

VI. Born: November 22, 1950. I'd say he's a sweet person, talks sweetly and thinks sweetly, perhaps idealistically. He probably likes to talk a lot, is jovial, likes people. He could be a good storyteller. Women like him.

A lot of energy. And he has the Saturn-Mars square found in a lot of boxers, so I would say he has power also.

EVENT: September 23, 1978. This is so complicated, I can't make a flat statement whether it was good or bad. But it was of great significance, because there were aspects after aspects (of the stars) hitting his chart that day. There could be something very surprising about this event.

Saturn is right on the edge of his House of Career. Saturn is the planet of the ending of things, so this was very significant in his career and his life.

Was he hurt, or could there have been anything involving a hospital in this situation?

There was something mysterious about this whole thing. It may be that he had a sense of mysterious things happening around him that he felt very strongly. I sort of lean to something very disappointing, but I can't quite back it up.

But there's a strong emphasis on hospitals and health.

Answers on page 138.

This essay was written in 1987.

ANSWERS TO *READING LIST*

I. October 1, 1932: Babe Ruth's "called the shot" home run
II. August 30, 1918: Ted Williams (I didn't give an event date)
III. October 5, 1951: Bobby Thomson's "shot heard round the world"
IV. August 1, 1978: Pete Rose's hit streak ends
V. October 18, 1977: Reggie Jackson's three World Series homers
VI. September 23, 1978: Lyman Bostock is shot to death.

Baseball and American Manhood

By MERRITT CLIFTON

ANALYSTS OF THE LATE 20TH CENTURY American male psyche often lament that our culture has abandoned traditional coming-of-age exercises, that our young men no longer receive a systematic initiation into the character requirements of manhood from their elders, completed by a recognition ceremony, and thus often reach adult age with little or no idea of how to fulfill the duties expected of men. The consequences of this failing seem to be self-evident in the number of single-parent families headed by women; the number of young men in prison (more, per capita, than in any other nation in the world); and the high suicide rate among young men who should be at their peak of optimism.

As poet Robert Bly and many others now repeatedly point out, we men seem to have either lost or abdicated our traditional responsibilities and identity. First there was the Industrial Revolution, which replaced small, decentralized, rural workplaces with factories and offices, instituting formal hierarchical management in place of the far more casual management structures of farms, where though the dominant male might have the final say, three generations often share the labor and have input into the decision making. The present symptoms of male malaise were already present in Britain's industrial centers by 1800, afflicting U.S. cities by 1850. Victorian morality and enforced temperance helped forestall the collapse of the traditional male role as defender and provider for a few generations, but the support structure of extended family fell away almost as quickly as men left farming for urban employment. In 1900, 80 percent of American men still lived and worked in the countryside; but by 1950, following 35 years of massive dislocation through grasshopper plagues, the Great Depression, the Dustbowl, and a series of wars, more than 90 percent had become urbanites. Men throughout the nation lost their old roles, and deliberate abandonment of the traditional male role coincided with the advent of the *Playboy* "philosophy" of hedonistic materialism in the mid-1950s. The abdication continued at an ever-accelerating pace through the so-called sexual revolution of the 1960s, which generally left women holding the same responsibilities as ever but with less male support. The evolution of female emancipation followed during the past two decades, when women, largely of necessity, developed their own support and survival networks; and the simultaneous rise of homosexuality to social acceptance, though centuries overdue, nonetheless further muddled familiar masculine roles.

According to the popular analysis, best articulated by Bly, young men today find themselves caught between two roles, neither of them comfortable: They can become feminized wimps, sensitive and caring, but afraid to be self-assertive and strong lest this be seen as chauvinistic behavior; or they can cling to the John Wayne warrior/hero image, now recast as the rootless Rambo, which rose out of men's post-Industrial Revolution search for identity in earlier hero myths that had originally served to warn men against such sins of the strong and brave as hubris (Oedipus, Roland), lust (Lancelot), and treachery (Tristan). Either way, young men aren't becoming themselves; or what most women want; or what society needs.

However, in looking for formalized tribal rituals, finding only the Bar Mitzvah surviving into the present age, the cultural anthropologists and others advancing this line of thought overlook the importance of sublimated ritual. Though our supposedly secular society superficially lacks the religious elements that helped structure life in earlier times, we do have three powerful competing male rites in the United States, more unique to our culture than is commonly supposed, each of which emerged coincidental with our transition from agrarian to urban living. And, as usual when a religion is driven underground, when something of psychic importance is repressed, these rites may be all the more influential for having evolved unrecognized.

Not that any of these religions—baseball, football, and sport hunting—actually go unseen by anyone. More than 15 million Americans of all ages play baseball or softball; more than 150 million watch baseball on television. Cultural commentators have referred to baseball as the American religion for well over a century, almost as long as the game has been called the Great American Pastime. Though football participation in any given year is far less than for baseball, no more than 1.5 million, most male Americans have played the game at some level; the television audience also pushes 100 million. Seldom analyzed as such, football, too, is commonly described as a quasi-religion. More than 14 million Americans hunt, down about six million during the past decade, but scarcely anyone is unaware of the gunfire. Once again, observers liken the activity to religion; once again, the metaphor is rarely extended beyond descriptions of the dedication with which participants pursue (or watch) their objective.

In each case, the influence these secular religions have upon the developing male psyche is almost entirely unexamined. And the examination, when it is done, tends to focus upon the superficial aspects: camaraderie, teamwork, maybe so-called male bonding. That any of these religions may be about the basic subjects of all recognized religions—sexuality and self-identity—seems to have escaped cultural investigators. (Two possible exceptions might be Mark Harris, who laid it out in his 1951 novel *The Southpaw*, and the crew who made the 1980 film *The Deer Hunter*, which was generally misconstrued as a film about the Vietnam War.)

Yet sexuality and the search for self-identity so pervade baseball, football, and hunting that once recognized at all, these aspects seem inescapable. In essence, these are three different ritualized paradigms of what makes a man a man, introduced to young men on the verge of puberty by older men. Each grows out of a tradition as old as civilization itself. Each tends to exclude women from active participation, not so much because of physical requirements—despite the pretense of most participants—as because the lessons taught are of primary importance to those who will inseminate women, not those who will bear the children.

Of the trio, hunting is commonly supposed to have evolved first, simply because the most primitive societies still extant are hunter/gatherer cultures. But archaeological and anthropological evidence suggests that even subsistence hunting developed from other needs than just food; our earliest known ancestors were primarily vegetarians, who dwelled in climates where the growing season never ended, where hunting was never either necessary or practical in terms of the effort expended to get a meal. The earliest known weapons were apparently designed for use against other humans, not animals. Indeed, hunting may have begun as a means of getting some economic return from the necessity of having a certain number of men from each tribe out beating the bush at all times to intercept hostile raiders—usually mate-seeking young men of nearby tribes. Thus, from the beginning, hunting may have had a sexual stimulus, intensified as men discovered that bringing home an edible carcass increased their stature with both fellow men and eligible women. A man's strength and courage were measured by the strength and courage of whatever he could kill.

By that time, humans may have already been swatting rocks with sticks and kicking their enemies' skulls about—the reputed beginnings of baseball and football. In any event, hunting for the greater part of recorded history has been primarily a pursuit enjoyed by the rich and powerful; peasants trapped and snared, but had neither the time, the access to land, nor the weapons to seek "game". Sport hunting as practiced by Americans is of uniquely American origin: a product of the first culture that had the weapons, the abundance of animals, the agricultural productivity, and the degree of social equality to permit it. In America, for the first time since civilization began, both animals and land were every man's for the taking. When both ran out, around the end of the 19th century, land grabs ceased (except via legal mechanisms) and hunting became regulated, but the paradigm for life (and death) that hunting had become continued.

According to the National Shooting Sports Federation, the average hunter starts at age 15, just past puberty, just before his first sexual experience, and is taught to hunt by older male family members. "It's like a Bar Mitzvah," one young hunter confirmed in an interview with *The Los Angeles Times*. "When you go deer hunting, they start to look at you as a man, and you feel like a man."

Why? Hinted Dave Petersen in *The Mother Earth News Beginner's Guide to Deer Hunting*: "Consider that the term *venison*, for the meat of the deer, is derived from the name of Venus, the Roman goddess of love. . . *venery* means both the art of hunting and the pursuit of sexual pleasure."

Subliminal confusion of hunting with sexual pleasure and achievement of manhood fairly gushes through hunting terminology, from the ritual of "first blood" to technical discussions of the penetration power of ammunition, to the frequent, casual, unconscious use of "her" (as in "I shot her right there") to describe male animals. Weapon-as-phallus is obvious symbolism, as is discharge-as-orgasm. The symbolic representation is strongest in deer hunting, the most popular kind of hunting. Even if hunters don't shoot deer to demonstrate sexual potency, or out of sexual frustration in lieu of raping and killing women, there can be little doubt that as a masculine rite, the real object is to kill the feminine in each hunter's self. The targets are predominantly male animals, but with the mythic feminine traits of grace and beauty. The pursuit requires sequestering the hunters, the men, away from female influence. Deer camp is an all male world. Instead of cleansing themselves as women require, as prelude to sexual contact, deer hunters cover themselves with "scent lures," a euphemism for urine and feces. They don't wash because detergent residues reflect ultraviolet light that deer can see, making camouflage useless. They wear boots indoors, curse, play poker, drink from the bottle, and eat from the can—and many never actually hunt at all, getting no closer to a deer than viewing a so-called "stag" video.

The atmosphere of exaggerated masculinity is not unlike that of "leather trade" gay bars. The lessons that young men cannot help but learn are that becoming a man requires repressing sensitivity and anything else that a man might have in common with women; that sex is violence; that men respect the "lady-killer," not the man who develops a mature, enduring relationship with someone who is a genuine partner rather than a mere objectified target of lust.

Football at the playing level likewise involves male sequestering and an atmosphere of exaggerated masculinity, but as sexual ritual it is about something else entirely. It is significant here that American-style football emerged from rugby, and that rugby, in turn, is the major sport of British boys' schools. Though the origins of both sports may be traced back to "kicking the Dane's head," or booting the skull of a fallen Viking through village streets in the Dark Ages, the sexual implications didn't begin to emerge until early Victorian times, when the shape of the ball and basic postures of the players first took modern form. To that point, the game had been but another of many, modeled on war, whose object is simply the conquest of territory. It was, and still is, a close cousin to chess, soccer, basketball, tennis, hockey, and polo. Such territorial games certainly have their own cultural connotations, and some of them also involve sexuality, as the players who are successful in penetrating enemy territory climax their conquest by propelling a ball or puck, symbolic sperm, into a goal—a passive feminine receptacle. None of these games, however, embody sexual symbolism in other major aspects. No one plays the feminine role; the goalie is only the old man left behind to guard home and hearth while the young men go out raiding. None of the players take overtly suggestive postures. The sexual act of scoring goals is preceded by combat among men, not by sexually enticing display or foreplay. Though soccer, hockey, and basketball have achieved significant popularity and fan devotion worldwide, they have not transcended sport—at least in this culture—to achieve quasi-religious stature. They remain, at root, variants of kicking the Dane's head.

When the ball, the Dane's head, was recreated in the shape of a turd, first rugby and later football broke away from the prototypical pattern to become the sports of anal fixation—of repressed sexuality to some degree, but of immature sexuality even more. The object became not just to conquer territory and rape the women who dwell there but also to smear one's own excrement on the opposition; to mark territory, much as cats and dogs do. (Consider that approximately half of each football game is occupied with simply measuring and marking the yardage, the ground marked by each play.) The struggle for dominance that characterizes all games thus became an overt struggle for sexual dominance, for access to females belonging to the opposition, soon symbolized—in America—not only by the passive goal, but also and perhaps even more by the provocatively dressed and highly active cheerleaders lined up behind each bench. The abstract female symbols of Queen and country apparently are enough for our stereotypically more repressed but possibly more sexually mature British counterparts.

Unlike hunting, football doesn't teach overt misogyny (though in the postures of center and quarterback at the beginning of each play, when the turd-shaped ball is passed between the center's legs, it may suggest buggery). But football does teach young men that women are prizes of war, to be won or lost; and it teaches that waging war is the object of life.

Baseball, by contrast, includes both masculine and feminine roles. It is a game in which the strongest, most masculine men—the pitcher and the catcher—are figuratively women; in which men must confront women who are not only their peers, but perhaps their superiors, and must earn respect not only by how well they swing their phallus, the bat, but also by their courage in standing up to the ever-present prospects of injury and failure. Though injury is actually rare, especially compared with football (only two professional baseball players have ever been killed by pitch balls, one in the major leagues in 1920, the other in the minors in 1949), it is nonetheless the ability to overcome instinctive terror of a hard object whistling past one's body as rapidly as someone else can throw it that truly separates the men, the hardball players, from the boys (of whatever age), who play softball. And it is attempting to hit that hard object, both speeding and changing parabolas in mid-flight, that helps men confront their own mortality. The recognition of each is inextricably linked to the desire to go beyond merely siring children to fathering them, as well; to pass something of one's self, as well as of one's genes, to posterity. The man who understands that even great hitters only make square contact three times in ten, and yet still tries on his own account, has begun to learn why and how it is that men must go on being men, even though the rewards of valor and dedication may be slight or none. Such a man has begun to learn how to be heroic, worthy of a woman—the pitcher for his own side—who will bear his young. Because acquired knowledge is at least as valuable in baseball as physical prowess, he has begun to learn, too, why fatherhood is at least as important as siring.

The allegories in baseball, as in all unconscious symbolism, are neither exact nor unilateral. Each facet of the game may mean one thing or many things, not necessarily in logical juxtaposition. The essentials, however, are that the pitcher, the fertile woman, serves her egg to the would-be inseminator, the batter, the man with the phallus; and that the game has nine innings, corresponding to the nine months of human gestation. Also of note are the roles of the catcher, a squatting midwife; the bullpen coach, who sequesters other pitchers in a symbolic harem; and the fielders, family of the pitcher on the mound, who protect her against the enemy rapists. As a fertile woman, the pitcher on the mound occupies an exalted position, a literal pedestal. Her arm is treated with all the superstition of a woman's sexual parts. Her role is projected to the point that in 1973, as women's liberation helped women adopt roles other than that of wife and mother, the American League, most minor leagues, and much of amateur baseball adopted the designated hitter rule, which prohibits pitchers from batting—from adopting the male role, even momentarily, hesitantly, experimentally, and ineptly. In baseball, a sport rooted in tradition more than any other, one must be male or female; one rarely can be both. Babe Ruth, who acquired a feminine nickname as a young pitcher, underwent a symbolic sex change in switching to the outfield to concentrate upon hitting.

Though no rule or physical impediment prevented him from continuing to pitch every fourth or fifth day, he pitched only nine games in his final fifteen seasons.

The pitcher flirts with the hitters, teasing with curves, tempting with fastballs. The hitters strive to get to first base, and eventually to score, two instances where slang metaphor has come to mean exactly what the subject subliminally does mean. This is the act of impregnation. The victorious pitcher is the one whose pregnancy goes the full distance (these days, usually with the help of a relief pitcher). The essence of the game lies in protecting the females of one's own tribe from the males of the other, while inseminating the females of the other.

Baseball, in short, is a fertility rite. Not by accident is it descended from a game, rounders, that was initially favored by English schoolgirls (who usually pitched, gently, to their own teammates, thereby avoiding the aspects of conquest that male players promptly introduced with the pitcher/batter conflict). Nor is it accidental that baseball became important in America just as the Industrial Revolution began to separate formerly agrarian Americans from fertility as a fact of life; that baseball briefly declined in favor of football in the 1960s, when the disproportionate size of the Baby Boom generation combined with the abdication of responsibilities by older men to put a disproportionate share of the population at the anal stage of sexual awareness; or that the ambivalence of male self-identity at present parallels the ambivalence of Americans toward baseball, which is now the sport that everyone watches but very few actually try to play in all its dangerous complexity. Young men today settle for softball, presenting no risk of injury to the batter from the sexually symbolic interaction with the pitcher, and little risk of striking out. Because there is neither danger nor acute risk of failure in softball, there is little opportunity for growth through playing it. Softball players may outgrow the anal fixation, may even learn to share the diamond with actual women as more-or-less equals, but they don't learn from the game how to be men.

Amateur baseball—participant baseball—also took a big wrong

turn with far-reaching implications for society with the advent of Little League, founded in 1939, but rising to national prominence only after World War II. Many amateur leagues existed before Little League, involving players of all ages, but except for those based on school rivalry reinforced by community rivalries and competition in other sports, most of them were relatively short-lived and unsuccessful. Although the American Amateur Baseball Congress, still extant, was founded in 1935, neither it nor any other amateur baseball association before the rise of Little League in the 1950s succeeded in establishing a nationwide league structure.

Little League succeeded for three reasons. First, due to the Baby Boom, a disproportionate share of the population was of the age to learn baseball. Second, the simultaneous emergence of television during that decade replaced the example of the successful town or company team with that of major league baseball. For the first time, most fans saw more of the major leagues than of ballgames in their own neighborhoods, and correspondingly amended their conception of how the game should be organized. Third, an entire generation of fathers, for the first time in U.S. history, had come of age through experience in an institutionalized context. Former generations had come of age through individual fortune-seeking: booking passage to America, going west, starting a farm or small business, becoming a hobo. Relatively few young men endured such rituals of passage at any given time. Rarely were the prevailing rituals attached to a collective or societal sense of purpose (which helped to prevent the rituals from being recognized as anything other than simply the act of growing up and assuming adult responsibility). Simultaneously, social convention throughout the first century and a half of U.S. nationhood tended to be highly structured, excluding young men from the possibility of desirable mating—marriage—until they had achieved economic status. The rapid rise of baseball during the middle of the Victorian era thus may have come at least partially from the subliminal appeal of a game in which intrepid individuals simultaneously took on the challenges of mating—hitting the pitcher—and of achieving status, against the opposition of the pitcher's already established and disdainful family, the fielders. The young men who came of age in the work camps of the Great Depression and World War II and Korean War military service necessarily had a different experience, developing a different outlook even from the veterans of World War I, a comparatively small group whose service was of much shorter duration, and those of the Civil War, who primarily fought with locally raised companies, alongside men they had known all their lives and would return home with, assuming they survived the war.

In particular, because the experience of the Great Depression and World War II generation was externally structured by government rather than community, this generation imagined that external governmental structure was an essential part of education in life. Because their experience was collective, their view of life, and baseball, tended to emphasize the primacy of the team rather than that of the individual; because the World War II and Korean War combat teams were not community based, as Civil War combat teams had been, notions of community began to be lost. The role of the team, for World War II veterans, was not to achieve either individual or communal goals (i.e., goals strengthening the sense of communal belonging), but to compete within a league of other teams: other armies. Since the model of success for armies is unconditional victory, and since the outcome of war tends to be shaped by politics, off-the-field politics as well as playing-field performance became an increasingly significant part of amateur baseball. Primarily, the politics were exercised by fathers, who assumed the role of military officers, sending their sons out to figurative war—whose outcome the fathers then tried to control through the introduction of umpires, uniforms, restrictions on who could and couldn't play, schedule manipulations, and sponsorships.

Such machinations and responses had always been prevalent in professional baseball, whose politics were initially Byzantine, through some sixty years of extreme league instability, and then Machiavellian, as the most powerful coterie of club owners evolved means of controlling the rest, the figurative nobility, and their mercenary armies, the players. But before Little League, professional baseball had always fundamentally differed in structure from amateur baseball—whose top players, with independent semi-pro and company teams, often were actually paid more (albeit unofficially) than most low-level professionals. Professional baseball adopted a league structure essentially because it was, and is, a cartel. Amateur baseball flourished without a league structure because unlike the members of the cartel, amateur teams had no special advantages to protect. Teams tended to draw talent either from their own communities, ranging from small towns to city blocks, or from sponsoring companies and organizations. Unlike professionals, the players were not formally bound to their teams; but also unlike professionals, they tended to remain with their teams year in, year out—unless, of course, they were both good enough and ambitious enough to turn professional. Although most teams had a designated manager, usually a veteran player or former player whose knowledge of baseball was generally respected, the teams tended to manage themselves for the most part, more or less collectively, much as family farms did. Opponents were drawn from surrounding towns and/or neighborhoods, and schedules were arranged a game or two at a time, so that if a team found itself overmatched at a given level of competition, it could quickly regroup against lesser teams. Conversely, stronger teams tended to seek stronger opponents. Either way, unlike professional counterparts, amateur teams rarely sacrificed their community bonds by replacing weaker players with outsiders (usually derided as "ringers"), and rarely disbanded from the humiliation of unrelieved losing.

Is the answer to the dilemma of American manhood that we should rediscover playing baseball? Perhaps; but only if we rediscover, as well, what made playing baseball an essential ritual for young-to-middle aged men in our agrarian past, when leisure time was so much scarcer (at least during the planting, haymaking, and harvest seasons) that one would suspect baseball should have held a lower priority then than now, and when merely watching baseball was the preferred pastime not of men in their prime, but of women, those too young to play, those too old, and the incapacitated.

First, amateur baseball must break free of the hierarchical structure characterizing professional baseball. At present, 2.5 million Little Leaguers are generally perceived—and perceive themselves—as the base of a pyramid in which only the best players go on to Pony League, only the best Pony Leaguers graduate to play in Colt League and Babe Ruth League, only the best of these play for their high schools, only the best high schoolers play at the American Legion level, and so forth, through college and the minor leagues, until at last the most elite of the elite emerge in the majors. Such an ever-narrowing structure not only tends to exclude millions of young men (and young women) from healthy recreation, it also excludes the young men from participating in a rite that—if conducted in the proper spirit—can help them become happier, healthier, better adjusted grown men.

The proper spirit is not competition in a league structure, or, indeed, in any structure at all, other than that of baseball itself. Young men (and those young women who want to play) must again be allowed to play what used to be called sandlot ball, with informal pickup teams, no uniforms, no umpires, no standings, no designated hitter rule to exclude players from full participation years before they even find out what their talents are, no rules to say someone can't play because his/her birthday falls a day or two (or year or two) on the wrong side of an arbitrary line, or because he or she moved into the neighborhood a day or two too recently. As young men mature physically, they must again have the opportunity to be initiated into the world of grown men by being allowed to play, as equals, with grown men. The presence on the diamond of a handful of older male authority figures—coaches and umpires, well removed from actual play—is no substitute for the presence of older brothers, neighbors, co-workers, even fathers, as fellow players, taking the same risks of failure and demonstrating, not just preaching, the lessons of courage, patience, forbearance, humility, and good sportsmanship. Grown men, too, must again dare to play baseball, must permit themselves to play baseball (and fail at it); not just send their sons out as often confused and reluctant surrogates.

To some extent, softball has evolved as a stand-in, a game

including many of the essential elements of baseball, which is still played on the sandlots (albeit less and less), and does include participants of all ages. But softball, too, has been massively co-opted by the influences of television, major league baseball organization, and league politics. Unlike a generation ago, most softball today is played in a league structure; and since all-time highs in participation were reached in the early 1980s, softball has followed amateur baseball into slow decline.

But even if the self-destructive organizational trend of softball could be reversed, it wouldn't replace the crying need of American men—young and old—for the personal confirmation that comes from standing up to an inside fastball, swallowing fear of either being hit or striking out, and being appreciated by peers both younger and older just for making the effort. With the possible exception of fastpitch, a softball variant closely resembling baseball of the mid-19th century, an underhand serve of a ball twice as large still only simulates the essential challenge of baseball. Nor can anything in softball pitching (other than fastpitch) fully replace the subliminal effect on a young man's mind of pitching a baseball, experiencing from inside out a feminine role *without* any self-consciousness about his gender.

We have—or should have—outgrown anything hunting can teach us. We should eventually outgrow football. Baseball, however, has elements that could be as enduringly instructive and helpful as any ritual of manhood having come before, if we learn once again to play the game instead of merely watching. For too many, perhaps 85 percent of young American males, intense attraction to baseball has already been reduced to just watching the game by the onset of puberty. It may not be wholly coincidence that the decline of participant baseball came not only simultaneous with the advent of television, but also with the advent of open sexual voyeurism, beginning with the publication of *Playboy* and expanding to the point that sex-oriented publications and videos are as ubiquitous as sports news. Despite loosening sexual mores and a quadrupling of sexual activity among teenagers since 1970, sex, too, seems to have become a pastime of observers more than of participants. Fear of

AIDS and other diseases, the high divorce rate (with the long lapses between relationships that follow most divorces, despite the stereotype of post-divorce promiscuity), and the exhaustion of the working single parent (usually female) are only a few of the many factors suggesting that even if part of the American population is having exponentially more sex than ever before, the majority suffer family lives and sex lives that if not worse than those of previous generations, are certainly not measurably more satisfactory.

Sandlot baseball won't heal bad relationships. It could even get in the way of relationships, much as league softball, jogging, golf, and especially televised football and hunting do now. What it could do, if multi-generational amateur play ever again transcends both vicarious observation and playing at being major leaguers, is help young men begin the process of self-appraisal, consultation, adjustment, and sacrifice, within the context of partnership, that enables mature grown men to make relationships work. As a ritual, uniquely organized around symbolic representatives of both the male and female members of the extended family, this is what baseball is all about. Hunting is about rape, football about immature sexuality; baseball, and baseball alone, goes beyond the rutting stage to teach men to be not only mates but also good husbands, and eventually, good examples for other men.

Baseball's Regional Character

By WILLIAM HUMBER

THINK OF BASEBALL as the Catholic Church. Rome asserts its authority through its leadership, imposed doctrine, and ability to dispense favors and power. Out in the territories, however, vibrant local chapters practice unique brands of liberation theology and accommodate peculiar local customs into the liturgy.

The forces of centralization struggle with the independence-minded regions in baseball as in religion. Right now head office is in the ascendancy. The ideology of baseball permeates our everyday life and at its center are the major leagues. No incongruity within the established order can be tolerated—not even Minnie Minoso having one at-bat in a minor league game.

Baseball's current status as an enormously popular form of mass entertainment hides to some extent the game's amazing and somewhat independent regional heritage. Indeed, within the lifetime of many of today's baseball fans a time can be recalled when regional features dominated the game. Ballplayers lived in the neighborhoods in which they played, an annual big league team attendance of one million was cause for civic rejoicing, minor leagues flourished as quasi-independent organizations employing career minor leaguers who never saw the daylight of a major league game, and barnstormers of major league ability filled small-town ballparks. While the popularity and worth of minor league baseball has never been greater than at present, there are already significant indications that the major leagues would like to impose more stringent economic controls over their feeder minor league systems.

Baseball's regional strength was built out of the formative efforts of local players and organizers. Unlike football, basketball and other sports that arose later, and under the harsher glare of the national media or national sporting organizations, baseball was incubated for a longer period in local communities. The game came to prominence in North America in the first half of the 19th century, metaphorically soaking itself like rain into the very soil of the continent's towns and villages. Across the landscape there appeared rough-cut diamonds and backstops which remain one of North America's clearest symbols of human settlement. The game was a regional activity, featuring local rules, players, and organization. Only gradually did the triumph of the New York rules version of the game in the 1850s, professionalization in the 1860s, and the rise of the majors in the 1870s allow a centralized forum for the game. Baseball's local and regional character, however, remained extremely resilient and has provided the game with a certain color and irony often lacking in the more antiseptic charms of the "one true way."

Consider the case of Canada. There are elements of the Canadian experience which in relation to the United States are akin to those of an American region. It has been idly assumed for years that the game's popularity and growth in Canada is a one-sided affair of Yankee promoters foisting their national treasure on a hapless and ill-prepared neighbor. This is a vision of trans-national determinism, however, that pays little heed to history.

First, baseball's identity as the great American game did not surface until after the Civil War. Even then it took decades of work on the part of entrepreneurs like Albert Spalding, culminating in the bogus assertion in 1906 that the game had been invented in Cooperstown, New York, in 1839, to solidify the claim.

Nor were American promoters very successful in transplanting the game to foreign locales. A crusading effort undertaken by Harry Wright in 1874 to bring baseball to Britain was a failure. Spalding's World Tour of 1889-90 left no discernible impact. While the game did catch on in places like Japan and the Caribbean, it was usually by accident or the result of locals watching missionaries or members of the armed forces play the novel game.

Interesting other countries in the game arose during what might be thought of as the second generation of baseball's rise to popularity in the United States—a period after the Civil War. Canadians participated in the first generation of baseball growth, and southwestern Ontario was, in fact, an important regional center that contributed to the game's evolution into the greater uniformity that would characterize baseball by 1860. The game played in this part of Canada—like that in Philadelphia, New York, and Massachusetts—had its own unique character and rules.

The story of baseball's first game in Canada, if not widely known to the American baseball public, is at least appreciated by the community of baseball scholars. Irving Leitner made one of the first references to the 1838 game in Beachville, Ontario, in his book *Diamonds in the Rough* (1971). I provided further details in my history of Canadian baseball, *Cheering for the Home Team* (1983), and Nancy Bouchier and Robert Barney put flesh and clothes on the bones of these accounts in their essay in *Baseball History* (1989). The events in summary form are as follows: On June 4, 1838, the traditional Military Muster Day and celebration of the King's Birthday in the British Empire, merchants and local farmers played a primitive form of early baseball in the small community of Beachville (about 40 miles southeast of present-day London, Ontario). Watching were troops of Scotch volunteers off to fight the remnants of rebel bands which a year earlier had attempted to overthrow the governing class of Upper Canada with its strong connections to the colony's British rulers. The rebels promoted a more popular democratic style of government based directly on American ideas and models.

The rebels failed in their quest. Many of their leaders, such as William Lyon MacKenzie, escaped to New York State, while others were transported to the penal colony in Australia. A few like Cornelius Cunningham, a Beachville wagon-maker, were executed. The rebellion itself was not surprising. For years Canadians had been warned about the spread of the American frontier into

Canadian territory. Prevalent fears of incipient Yankeeism were voiced. American settlers moving west used the Niagara-to-Detroit route through southern Ontario as a shortcut. Many of them, like the parents of those who had played in the Beachville game, simply decided that here was a good place to settle.

The Canadians who played baseball had no idea that they were playing one of the great symbols of American culture. Nor was there such thought on the part of the spectators. Before the American Civil War baseball was not a form of popular entertainment identified with any one country. It was a regional affair which owed its allegiance not to Abner Doubleday but to the game's more antique origins in northern European fertility rites welcoming back the spring season and to its more recent fossilization in Great Britain. In the 18th century, cricket emerged as the dominant bat and ball game played by adults in the British Isles. All other similar games, like knur and spell, stoolball, rounders, and so on, were arrested in their development, and came to be viewed as child's play. Jane Austen already recognizes baseball as a children's game in *Northanger Abbey,* which was released in 1798. And even today pompous but historically ignorant Brits scoff at baseball as nothing more than a girls' exercise played at beachside resorts on bank holidays.

The game, like so much of British culture, crossed the ocean into North America with the earliest settlers. References to it are found in the journals of Revolutionary War soldiers who would not have been much above the age of childhood. In the more open society of North America there were fewer cultural obstacles to prevent adults from bumbling around in what the more socially conscious Anglos might consider juvenile behavior. The early 19th century game of townball played on town meeting days in New England was an historic parallel to baseball's village play in England in the Middle Ages.

Historian Melvin Adelman (1980, 1986) has diagnosed baseball's ascendancy over cricket as a matter of North Americans choosing to play the game which at the time required weaker bat-and-ball skills. Quite simply, Americans weren't good enough to play cricket against English emigrants. As well, the English were not going to change the rules of their game to accommodate American complaints that the shift from offense to defense was not frequent enough to satisfy their demand for action. Accordingly, in the period leading up to the Civil War, American ballplayers adopted the easier-to-play of the two bat-and-ball games available and gave it a uniquely American definition even as they developed stronger and more "manly" bat-and-ball skills. They modernized a rough-hewn game by giving it rules and an organizational structure. They legitimized it as a game adults could play. And they established the foundation upon which major league baseball would arise.

The game played in Beachville in June of 1838 and in nearby towns was the somewhat primitive townball. (Granted it had been brought in by Americans but these players were people neither self conscious of the game's national origins nor aware of its real roots in Europe.) Dr. Adam Ford's account of the game appeared in the *Philadelphia Sporting Life* almost 50 years later. The names he recorded were all well known in the region. The specifics of play correspond to other types of baseball played in this era. The authenticity of his account suffers only because it is too detailed, suggesting that he added his own later understanding of the game's evolution to his childhood memories of that day. While Barney and Bouchier (1989) suggest the game may have been a kind of missing link between Cartwright's game of the mid 1840s and primitive townball, it was probably in fact no different from hundreds of other variants played in a multitude of isolated counties. What it had of true significance was the witness of a skilled narrator.

In southwestern Ontario, the informal play that appeared in the late 1830s evolved into formal baseball social organizations by the 1850s, less than 10 years after the "coming out' of the Knickerbockers in New York City. Bill Shuttleworth, a Hamilton clerk (1833-1903), organized Canada's first team, The Hamilton Young Canadians (later called the Maple Leafs). They played their intersquad games on the grounds facing Central School between Bond and Beverly Streets in Hamilton, beginning in 1854.

Shuttleworth's fellow players were a cross section of Hamilton's working population and included five clerks, three shoemakers, two turners, two laborers and, among others, a coach manufacturer, saloon keeper, hammerman, horse collar maker, cigarmaker, carpenter, sailor, and wool sorter.

About 100 miles west of Hamilton, near the village of Beachville, the emerging city of London, Ontario, recorded its first baseball team in George Railton's *London Directory* in 1856. Membership was restricted to 22 men so that they could be easily divided into two teams of eleven each. This game clearly differed from the New York version with its rule of nine on a side. And even in comparison to the Massachusetts version of the game, which allowed 10 to 14 on the field, the Canadian game was more proscriptive, strictly calling for 11 afield. As well, the Canadian game required all 11 players to be retired before the other team batted, as opposed to a Massachusetts requirement that only one be retired. Both games, however, allowed the pitcher to throw the ball in the modern style, rather than underarm, as specified in the New York rules. The additional positions in the Canadian game were a fourth baseman and a backstop behind the catcher.

While the major sporting weekly of the era, the *New York Clipper*, does not appear to have ever referred to this form of the game in southwestern Ontario by the explicit definition of "Canadian game," it was common for the publication to be this specific when covering New York, Massachusetts, and Philadelphia games. In its August 4, 1860 edition the *Clipper* notes that, "The game played in Canada differs somewhat from the New York game, the ball being thrown instead of pitched and an inning is not concluded until all are out. There are also 11 players on each side."

The Canadian brand of baseball remained popular in Ontario until the end of the 1850s, as did the practice of playing games only against the members of one's club and not against other teams or towns. South of the border, however, teams like the Brooklyn Atlantics, with their blue collar supporters, and their rivals the Excelsiors, supported by merchants and clerks, had begun to define a new style of play, increasingly remote from the easygoing fraternal character of earlier days. By the late 1850s, large, unruly crowds were common. Gentlemanly ideas gave way to more vibrant encounters, as the sport became the focus for occupational groups or rival communities eager to promote their name and pride beyond their civic borders. And it was in places like saloons, cigar stores, pool halls, and bookmaking establishments—the general hangouts of street-corner society—that the modern form of baseball emerged.

There was something about the New York rules (which are essentially those of today) which appealed to players and spectators alike. For one thing, they offered a quicker exchange between offense and defense. For another, they were codified, not subject to regional interpretation, and this made inter-squad and inter-town matches easier to organize. New York's general reputation as a cultural trendsetter further enhanced its power to direct baseball's future.

With the completion of the Great Western Railway, Britain's 1849 repeal of the Navigation Acts (which ended Canada's favorable trading position within the Empire), and the introduction of free trade between Canada and the United States in 1855, Canadians, particularly those in southwestern Ontario, were in constant contact with their American neighbor.

The use of the New York rules in Canada corresponds with the first mention of a game between teams representing rival cities. The Toronto Young Canadians defeated the Hamilton Young Americans 68-41 on May 24, 1859, the score being inflated by a lack of gloves, the players' poor skills, and the hitter's ability to designate where he wanted the ball tossed.

It was the Hamilton Burlingtons' loss to the Niagaras of Buffalo in 1860 in the first ever international baseball match which sealed the fate of the Canadian game. Buffalo had adopted the New York rules in 1857 and the pragmatic young merchants and businessmen of the Burlington club (formed in 1855 with 50 members and three meetings per week) willingly made the switch. The Hamilton Maple Leafs (formerly the Young Canadians) debated the merits of the new rules. Arthur Feast, a stonemason, who was to popularize the game in Guelph, supported Bill Shuttleworth's defense of the Canadian game; however, Charles Wood, a young innkeeper from the United States, won the day with his support of the New York game.

In Woodstock (near London), Bill's younger brother Jim Shuttleworth organized a team in 1860. They retained the Canadian rules and defeated the Rough and Ready Club of Ingersoll twice that year. By the next year, though, Charles Wood had convinced them to switch to the New York game, and the Canadian game, as such, disappeared. It is worth noting that even in switching to the New York game, Canadian organizers retained certain unique interpretations of the rules much as the Canadian Football League does today in comparison to the NFL. Canadian baseball's uniqueness lasted until the 1876 season when the newly formed Canadian Association brought itself in line with the National League. "It has been found," London newspaperman Harry Gorman said, "that the rules regarding 'called balls' and 'strikes' are too favorable to the batter, and that Canadian games, as a consequence, do not compare on record with American games of the same class, played under American rules. Playing under different rules also leads to confusion, and a change is desirable."

It might be concluded that the exit of rule differentiation formally ended the regional character of the game in Canada. But such a conclusion would then also lead one to assume that regionalism disappeared as a factor in baseball's growth in the United States. Nothing, of course, could be further from the truth. And indeed it would require far more study and time than this essay to explore this far-reaching topic. One looks largely in vain in popular baseball literature for much discussion of this theme, although many books have done an admirable job of chronicling baseball's regional beginnings. One thinks of, among others, James Bready's *The Home Team* on Baseball in Baltimore, Wheeler and Baskin's *The Cincinnati Game*, Louis Cauz's *Baseball's Back in Town* on baseball in Toronto, and Joe Overfield's *The 100 Seasons of Buffalo Baseball*. There needs to be more analysis, however, of the significance of these regional threads in baseball's greater story.

In Canada, more specifically southwestern Ontario, the period between 1860 and 1890 was a time of tremendous baseball development. Local entrepreneurs like brewer George Sleeman put Guelph on the baseball map, while in London, the local Tecumsehs won arguably Canada's only major league baseball title as 1877 pennant winners of the International Association, the first major rival to the National League. In the face of significant professionalization and the arrival of many Americans to play on teams in London, Guelph, Hamilton and Toronto, young Canadian lads like Tip O'Neill and Bob Emslie nevertheless emerged as stars in the American major leagues in the 1880s.

Local officials could always be found to give a peculiar twist to some of baseball's ongoing conundrums. For instance, the vigilant Board of Health in Woodstock, Ontario, banned the spitball around the turn of the century after concluding that it might pass on tuberculosis. A major report on the Americanization of Canada released in 1905 speculated that the country was in danger of losing its independence because of Canadian eagerness to bypass cricket and lacrosse in favor of baseball. The reporters never seemed to grasp the ways in which Canadians participated and contributed to baseball's evolution.

It is only possible to understand the Toronto Blue Jays' ability to attract four million spectators in the 1991 season by putting it in the context of the game's heritage in this part of Ontario. And further the Jays and Montreal Expos retain Canadian scouting bureaus not so much because the next Babe Ruth may be hidden in Moose Jaw but as a symbol, however little understood, that it is important not only to respect but to promote baseball's regional character. This in turn suggests that if the game turns away from its regional character, believing that it has a mass cultural support that transcends local values, it will eventually lose the base from which that support flows. It might be argued that baseball's temporary decline in the 1960s was caused in part by the Dodgers' move out of Brooklyn, where the impact of the region on baseball was particularly evident. Baseball executives might keep this in mind as they contemplate the future of the game in some of their smaller markets and as they redesign the traditional framework of baseball playoffs to suit national television contracts.

References

Adelman, Melvin. *A Sporting Time: New York City and the Rise of Modern Athletics*. Chicago and Champaign-Urbana: University of Illinois Press, 1986.

Barney, Robert Knight. "Diamond Rituals: Baseball in Canadian Culture" in *Baseball History 2* (Edited by Peter Levine). Westport, Connecticut: Meckler Books, 1989, 1-21.

Bready, James. *The Home Team: A Patriotic Story of Baseball in Baltimore*. Baltimore: Self-published, 1958.

Cauz, Louis. *Baseball's Back in Town: A History of Baseball in Toronto*. Toronto: Controlled Media Corporation, 1977.

Humber, William. *Cheering for the Home Team: The Story of Baseball in Canada*. Erin, Ontario: Boston Mills Press, 1983.

Landon, Fred. *Western Ontario and the American Frontier*. Toronto: Ryerson Press, 1941.

Leitner, Irving. *Baseball: Diamond in the Rough*. New York: Criterion Books, 1972.

Overfield, Joseph. *The 100 Seasons of Buffalo Baseball*. Kenmore, New York: Partners' Press, 1985.

Palmer, Bryan D. *A Culture in Conflict: Skilled Workers and Industrial Capitalism in Hamilton, Ontario — 1860-1914*. Montreal: McGill-Queen's University Press, 1979.

Vincent, Ted. *Mudville's Revenge: The Rise and Fall of American Sport*. New York: Seaview Books, 1981.

Wheeler, Lonnie and John Baskin. *The Cincinnati Game*. Wilmington, Ohio: Orange Frazer Press, 1988.

Thank God for Nuts—They Flavor the Game

By DAVID Q. VOIGT

AMERICA'S ENDURING flirtation with major league baseball still challenges students of national character to try to explain the phenomenon. After all, a typical game offers as little as ten minutes of action during its two-and-one-half-hour course. Obviously other factors must invigorate the spectacle. Not the least of these are the antics of the ubiquitous nuts who are counted among the few constants in the known universe. By their antics they enrich the game and contribute mightily to the dynamic flow of American humor.

Like the populace that wallows in it, American humor resembles a crazy quilt of diversity which shows few signs of merging into a singular form. Ever mixing and growing, the flood of American humor gains strength from media revolutions which have augmented spoken discourse with publications and broadcasts, thus lending credence to the late Marshall McLuhan's punning observation that the medium provides the massage!

Ever roiling in the flood of American humor is a whirlpool of nutty behavior. Indeed nuts are almost as old as American society. Until 1800, according to Eric Partridge's *Dictionary of American Slang*, the word "nuts" designated commendable zealous behavior on the part of targeted individuals. By 1858 the term had come to denote wrongheaded behavior. But major league baseball owes plenty to its nuts. This was a point well grasped by the late baseball historian Lee Allen, whose loving recollections of the game's nutty characters included the benediction, "Thank God for Nuts."

Baseball's history is dotted with memorable nutty episodes that have found their place in the humorous folklore of America. What aficionado has not heard of the Cleveland Wanderers of 1899, losers of 134 games? Or of the 239 errors committed by the 1930 Phillies? Or Bonehead Fred Merkle's failure to touch second base that contributed to the Giants' narrow defeat in the 1908 pennant race? Or Babe Ruth's still-debated called-shot homer in the 1932 World Series? Or the miracle Giant victory of 1951, an event that triggered joyous rioting at the Polo Grounds with one loving couple shucking off taboos and copulating in one of the box seats! And in 1983 the Yankees-Royals "Pine Tar" incident unleashed emotions that spilled into a New York appellate court, threatened counteraction from organized umpires and saddled the Yankee owner with a hefty fine for importunate remarks.

In its time each such incident seemed portentous and calamitous, but soon each was perceived as but another of the "silly season" episodes that dot baseball history. As such they become humorous sagas to be told and retold before gatherings of fans.

While designated nuts crop up among the game's heroes and villains, their natural habitat is in the ranks of the fools. As engagingly analyzed by sociologist Orrin E. Klapp, the fool is institutionalized in all major cultures, serving such useful functions as sublimating aggression, releasing tensions, maintaining social control and binding people into communities of laughter. In our highly diverse American society, Klapp dredged up at least twenty-five subtypes of fools which he lumped into five major categories. These categories are incompetents or ludicrous role failures (like baseball's bonehead Merkle), discounting types who serve to deflate authoritarians (like notorious umpire baiters), nonconformist types (like Alex Johnson refusing to run out ground balls), overconformers (like Ted Williams, who busted more than one hotel room mirror while practicing his swing), and comic butts or jesters (like Tug McGraw, who parried a prying reporter's question on how he spent his salary by quipping, "Ninety percent I spend on broads and Irish whiskey; the other ten percent I probably waste!")

Klapp's categories make a handy road map for chasing down and sampling baseball's nutty characters. While time and space limits insure notable omissions, the following "kook's tour" can provide a panoramic view of baseball nuts that could inspire more extensive foraging.

1. The Main Grove—the Player Nuts

In numbers and notoriety, nuts from the ranks of major league players lead all other constituencies of baseball. Among players branded as ludicrous role failures none tops the opprobrium heaped on "bonehead" Fred Merkle for failing to touch second base in a crucial 1908 game. But Merkle's all-round first base play was never questioned, which was not the case with latter-day first sackers like Zeke Bonura and Dick "Dr. Strangeglove" Stuart, who rank high in the annals of stone-fingered ineptitude. "Marvelous Marv" Throneberry cashed in on his dubious reputation with a lucrative pact for doing commercials for a beer company; Marv joined other ex-athletes turned barfly touts, including catcher Bob Uecker, who transcended a six-season .200 batting average.

Any player is fated to perform ludicrously somewhere along the line. Awesome virtuosos like Warren Spahn and Joe DiMaggio had off-moments at the bargaining tables. Spahn once opted for a straight salary of $25,000 over a club offer of ten cents for each paying fan; that blunder cost him an estimated pay of $182,000 for 1953! A similar choice once cost DiMaggio an estimated $50,000 in extra pay.

A truly far-out, ludicrous performance led Braves' pitcher Pascual Perez to be dubbed "Wrong Way Pascual" in 1982. Slated to pitch at Atlanta Stadium, this Dominican rookie got lost on Atlanta's freeway system and circled the city three times before running out of gas. Yet Pascual's "lost patrol" performance was credited with jollying the slumping Braves out of a losing streak as the much-kidded Pascual, wearing "I-285" on his warmup jacket, later won four games in the team's stretch drive to a divisional championship.

A second Klapp category, that of discounting types, features the kind of nuts who grow in a society where sham, braggadocio, phony behavior and false fronting abound. In his time "King" Kelly was as notorious a braggart as in our time was Reggie ("I'm the straw that stirs the drink!") Jackson. However, both managed to match big mouths with big deeds. This was less true of Art Shires, the self-styled "Arthur the Great" who joined the 1928 White Sox saying: "So this is the great American League . . . I'll hit .400." For a time the posturing Shires did well enough, but he never played a full season. Even in his fourth and final season he brashly sent a telegram of acceptance to the Boston Braves which he signed, "Your latest sensation." In 82 games he hit .238.

Such effrontery was exceeded by Ken "Hawk" Harrelson, an overrated slugger of the 1960s and later a vice-president of the White Sox, who gained notoriety as a bucker of baseball's conservative dress code by affecting long hair, batting gloves, sweatbands and flamboyant dress. Although denounced as a fop, Harrelson saw his reputation grow when he defied A's owner Charley Finley, who cut him loose. To Finley's discomfiture Harrelson sold his dubious services to the Red Sox in 1968 for a $75,000 bonus.

If player poseurs like these are themselves deflatable, Babe Ruth's ability to puncture the stuffed shirts of bigwigs had fans laughing with him rather than at him. On meeting Field Marshal Ferdinand Foch at Yankee Stadium, Ruth blithely quipped, "Hiya, Gen, I heard you were in the war!" On another occasion, on meeting President Calvin Coolidge at the Stadium he commented, "Hot as Hell, ain't it, Pres?" While such examples of *lèse majesté* are Olympian, Pete Rose's flip response to the congratulatory phone call from President Jimmy Carter at the close of the 1980 World Series is worthy of the genre. But anyone out to top Ruth in the debunking department would have to go *all* the way; indeed, Ruth helped to debunk his own funeral. Surely he'd have loved this exchange between his pall-bearing buddies Joe Dugan and Waite Hoyt. While serving at the funeral on that steamy day in 1948, Hoyt allowed that he could use a beer. "So could the Babe," quipped Dugan.

As a transgressor of societal norms, Ruth was a giant; his hearty appetite for wenching and carousing evokes astonishing gasps even in this hedonistic and revelatory age. In Ruth's time bowdlerizing reporters tidied up mention of many of his excesses, but enough seeped through to astonish even now.

Freer attitudes towards sex now lighten the onus placed on taboo violators, but autobiographical revelations from the pens of players like Jim Bouton, Bo Belinsky, Kirby Higbe and Joe Pepitone caused them to be shunned by other ballplayers. Proof may be seen by the stormy reception that greeted Bouton's blockbusting *Ball Four*. To this day Bouton is *persona non grata* at Yankee old-timer games, but his celebrity status in part dates from the book's appearance.

The sorriest of all player deviants would probably be the accused game-fixers and gamblers. In this shady enterprise the eight damned Black Sox stand alone, but baseball history is pock-marked with names of others like Jim Devlin, umpire Dick Higham, Hal Chase and more recently Denny McLain and numerous drug abusers.

The most memorable of nutty nonconformists may be those players who under game pressures express their frustration creatively. Thus, when outfielder Frenchy Bordagary concluded an argument with an ump by spitting in the official's eye, he was fined $500 and suspended. As Frenchy ruefully lamented, "The penalty is a little more than I expectorated." But that spitter was out-gobbed by Ted Williams, who on multiple occasions spat in the direction of heckling fans or the Fenway Park pressbox. In retaliation Boston writers hung the label of "The Splendid Spitter" on Ted.

In a career-long feud with his critics, Williams refused to doff his cap when applauded and at times vented frustrations by signaling hecklers with obscene finger gestures. Once, he angrily flung his bat into the stands and it happened to hit owner Tom Yawkey's housekeeper. For that and other outbursts Ted was targeted as a towering nonconformist. At other times he was considered a towering conformer. Such was Williams' range!

In the category of overconformers Ty Cobb loomed large. His

mania to be best fueled both his greatness and his alienation. On and off the field he was driven; once, upon returning to his hotel room and finding that his roommate had beaten him to the bathtub, he flew into a rage. Later he explained, "Don't you see, I have to be first in everything." Nor did he mellow much after his career had ended.

Hard-driving players risk being branded special sorts of nuts. Thus, Pete Rose's "Charley Hustle" exertions evoke admiration and jeers. To an extent so did Steve Carlton's stoical training, which included stuffing his left arm in a vat of rice, sometimes choosing his own catcher, stuffing his ears with cotton when pitching and refusing to communicate with the media. Of course nonconformists come in varied sorts. Rogers Hornsby eschewed movies lest they damage his batting eye, but steadfastly insisted on frequenting race tracks in defiance of Commissioner Landis' edict.

But some overconformers manage to enthrall fans. One, pitcher Mark Fidrych, became America's beloved "bird" (named after "Sesame Street's" Big Bird). In 1976, Fidrych's antics of talking to the ball, tidying up the mound and darting about thanking teammates after each win charmed fans. When interviewed at the end of his great season, Fidrych gushed, "I'm just loving it . . . what a dream!" Of his charisma his manager said, "Babe Ruth didn't cause this much excitement in his brightest day." Although that is debatable, Fidrych's appeal stemmed from an artful blending of over- and nonconformity. Thus, on meeting President Gerald Ford, he asked that worthy if he could get his son to fix him up with a date.

Today jesters and comic butts seem to get lumped together as "flakes," but baseball's broad historical landscape is dotted with unique zanies. Thus, who can forget Germany Schaefer, a turn-of-the-century speedster, stealing second base and then stealing first and being credited with another steal? His ploy had legislators speedily passing a rule forbidding such retreats. Or how about Gabby Street amazing a 1908 crowd by catching a ball which fell 555 feet from the Washington Monument? Ironically, Hank Helf of the 1940 Cleveland Indians caught one dropped from 700 feet and earlier on another Indian, Joe Sprinz, suffered a fracture of the jaw trying to catch an 800-foot drop—but only Street's feat is remembered. Or Lefty Gomez in a bases-loaded situation fielding a ball and tossing it to second baseman Tony Lazzeri, who had no play? Asked why, "Goofy" Gomez replied that he had been reading in the papers about what a smart player Lazzeri was!

At any time practical jokers infest clubhouses, dugouts and bullpens. Among the more notorious was reliever Moe Drabowsky, who used the bullpen phone to order pizzas and sometimes to falsely alert enemy relievers to get warmed up. In the Cardinal clubhouse Walker Cooper once managed to tie a mate's sweatshirt into twenty-five knots and Del Rice was the master of nailing shoes to floors. Elsewhere, there was Sparky Lyle imprinting his buttocks on the icing of a birthday cake, and Doug Rader picking his nose and planting the detritus on a nearby bare arm.

That such antics now are recorded in newspapers and magazines testifies to changing norms in American society. But if present standards admit grosser forms of behavior, the same standards appear less tolerant towards rule breakers or hecklers. Some observers have noted a recent decline in bench jockeying which they blame on the player union movement; supposedly brotherhood has added an environment of "legislated courtesy."

Because ballplayers always have lived highly pressurized lives, it is not surprising that some display symptoms of mental illness; indeed, it is a tribute to human resilience that so many adapt to the major league pressure cooker. But woebetide one who displays symptoms of mental illness, as our civilization is not that far removed from the days when inmates of Bedlam were objects of public gawking and ridicule.

Thus, the suicides of players like Marty Bergen, Chick Stahl and Willard Hershberger loom darkly in baseball history and are still topics of gossip. To a lesser extent gossip and ridicule are still heaped on players with known or suspected symptoms of mental illness. In the case of outfielder Jimmy Piersall such antics as running the bases backwards and climbing backstops were ridiculed and fans and enemy dugouts labeled him "nutsy"; later, when his condition became known, his ordeal was received with mixed bad taste and understanding in a book and a movie. Today the stigmatized Piersall is still viewed as a head case; his dismissal from an announcer's job dredged up past examples of his quirky behavior.

Other players with milder symptoms played under the same shadows. Included are pitchers like Steve Blass, whose inability to find the plate ended his career; Steve Dalkowski, whose awesome promise as a fireballer ended in the minors for similar reasons, and Kevin Saucier, who had a fear of hitting batters that made him fearful of going to the park and forced his recent retirement at age 27.

Undoubtedly there are others who conceal their symptoms. For this, blame the societal taboo on mental illness which has many Americans so fearful of exposure that they refuse to draw on medical policies to pay for symptom treatment. And even if ballclubs now provide paid therapy, the strains of exposure still pose formidable obstacles.

On the whole the brighter side eclipses the seamy side in the world of nutty behavior. The word *nut* is such a generalized catchword that nearly everyone has been on its receiving end at some time. Mostly the term evokes laughter and therein it is a source of strength for baseball. Moreover, players are by no means the only designated nuts as the game's other constituencies provide enough cases to deflect attention toward fans, owners, umps, media people and other auxiliaries of major league baseball.

2. The Peripheral Groves

A. Shaking the Managerial Tree

Any fan out to gather nuts in May will find good pickings among baseball's managers. In the early years bluff Cap Anson was targeted by fans because of his size and his aggressive, umpire-baiting style. As Anson grew older fans dubbed him "Unk," "Pappy" and "Grandpa" among other hoary terms. In retaliation, Anson once donned a long white beard and wore it during a game, performing well despite the prop and accompanying jeers. Yet fans never ceased ragging the big man, and his passing from the baseball scene left a noticeable gap.

Early in this century a new target, burdened with an even greater Napoleonic complex, appeared in the person of John McGraw. Like Anson, McGraw was targeted by fans everywhere. Some of McGraw's shrewd ploys, like the time he pinched one of his players to authenticate a hit-by-pitch claim, had fans screaming "Muggsy," an epithet he despised. When he loudly berated his 1916 team for quitting, home fans joined the chorus. So did his one-time buddy, then the victorious Dodger manager Wilbert Robinson.

By then Robinson's own nutty credentials were well established. His excess poundage had writers and fans calling him the "Round Robin" and chortling over his earlier attempt to catch a ball dropped from an airplane. Circling under the missile, the roly-poly ex-catcher got the heel of his glove on the missile, which deflected it into his chest. The blow felled him, and as he beheld his spattered chest, Robinson screamed, "I'm dead! I'm covered with blood!" But then, to his chagrin, he learned that the "ball" was really a burst grapefruit!

Similar charges of nutty incompetence dogged Casey Stengel for years—charges Stengel deflected by playing the role of comic jester. One of his more famous capers had him tipping his cap toward fans and releasing a captive bird. Later, as a winning Yankee manager and as a horrendous loser with the 1962 Mets, his mastery of confusing rhetoric charmed fans, even if they knew they were being conned. "We're a fraud," Stengel admitted after a defeat, adding, "the attendance got trimmed again."

Fans responded to nutty jester types like Stengel and his successor Yogi Berra. As a player Berra was already a celebrated malaprop, one who when roused out of bed by a phone call responded to the apologetic caller by saying, "That's okay. I had to get up to answer the phone anyhow." In actuality, Berra is not a very funny character, but like the Hollywood starlet he, too, was made to fit the part.

Of course, it's tough being a manager. Whatever one's style the manager is a sure bet to be blamed for losses and targeted as some kind of nut. Knowing this, one can imagine ordinary managers thanking the gods that a towering nut like Billy Martin was around to take up much of the flak. His antics like feuding with players, sometimes punching them out, or kicking dust over umps are well known.

B. The Owners

Unlike dumped-on managers, baseball owners are better shielded from accusing critics. Still, baseball history is dotted with owner nuts. In the judgment of some financiers, being a baseball owner is being a foolish investor; that so many opt to do so may suggest that they are seeking self-aggrandizement.

The list of nutty owners in baseball history is long. Let's begin with Chris von der Ahe, the legendary owner of the St. Louis Browns who became the comic butt of so many funny Dutchman stories in the 1880s and '90s.

Echoes of von der Ahe's style characterized modern owners like Bill Veeck and Charley Finley. As a promoter Veeck's ability to charm fans was proved during four separate stints as a club owner. One of these included a hopeless stint with the St. Louis Browns which saw Veeck cut a legendary caper by signing and sending to bat midget (43" tall) Eddie Gaedel, armed with toy bat and wearing uniform No. 1/8. Such stunts, mingled with a solid knowledge of baseball, endeared the pixie-like Veeck to fans and cast him as a lovable folk character.

Not so with Charles Oscar Finley, whose erratic behavior cast him as a petulant nut. Although brilliantly successful at times, Finley lacked Veeck's comic genius. Such Finleyesque ploys as bribing his men to wear beards and mustaches, decking them in garishly-colored uniforms, plumping for orange-colored bases and balls, designating a mule as the team totem and coining corny nicknames were laboriously contrived; often as not they had fans laughing at the owner rather than with him.

Erratic behavior also characterizes incumbent owners Ted Turner and George Steinbrenner. Turner's nutty qualifications stem from his jousts with former Commissioner Bowie Kuhn, who fined Turner for tampering with other team's players and who sternly ended the Atlanta owner's quixotic attempt to function as field manager. And a Turner decision to evict the team totem, Chief Noc-A-Homa, from his wigwam in order to add more seats in 1982 and again in 1983 was followed each year by a serious losing streak. That caper cast Turner as the nut who brought down Noc-A-Homa's curse!

Happily for Turner, whose prowess as a yachtsman was redeeming, there was also the mighty presence of Steinbrenner to overshadow his foibles as a baseball owner. The Yankee boss has won his spurs as the terrible-tempered Mr. Bang among owners by virtue of his frenzied spending at player auctions and his penchant for meddling in team affairs, for firing underlings (reportedly including a secretary for ordering a wrong kind of sandwich), and for dueling with officials. A decade of this stormy petrel caused a *New York Times* scribe to explode with this advice: "Go away, please, and take your favorite manager with you."

Among owners vilified as meddling nuts Steinbrenner stands tall in baseball history, but at times nearly every owner has been targeted. Thus, reclusive Phil Wrigley's stubborn refusal to light up Wrigley Field, his team's woeful performance since 1945 and such abortive innovations as replacing the manager with a system of rotating coaches helped to certify this late owner. And the roll call of situational nuts among owners included cash-poor types like Gerry Nugent of the Phillies, who ran the club as a parasite team; Judge Emil Fuchs, whose pinchpenny practices at Boston extended to his personally chasing foul balls hit into the stands; Clark Griffith of the Senators, who once sold son-in-law Joe Cronin to make money.

C. The Umpires

If being a club owner facilitates one's nutty reputation, consider the lot of the umpire. From the moment these officials take the field to choruses of ritualized boos their competence is called into question. And once at work hardly a game is played without someone challenging their mental togetherness. Among the plenteous examples, umpire Red Jones used to bristle at being called "Meat"; to his surprise he was targeted by orchestrated jeers from the White Sox bench which sounded, "We can't call you 'Meat' today," and the refrain quickly followed, "because it's Friday!" Then there was Beans Reardon, who was asked by a catcher how he managed to get his square head into a round mask, and plate ump Bill McGowan asking Nick Altrock what happened to the woman who was being carried from the stands on a stretcher and getting in reply, "You called one right and she fainted."

As baseball's ready-made villains, umps have long been cast as comic butts. But occasionally they fight back, as when one visited the hospitalized Leo Durocher; asked why he came to visit that notorious umpire baiter, the ump replied, "I came to see if you were dying."

D. The Media

That so many yarns become part of baseball's folklore owes to the game's vital media constituency. While free publicity has always been a powerful support for baseball, media men have also titillated fans with exposes of baseball's madcap sides.

As myth-makers generations of sportswriters coined and tagged players with nicknames like "Little Napoleon," "The Duke of Tralee," "The Colossus of Clout" and "The Georgia Peach." And always there were snide labels like "The Splendid Spitter" which helped tag players as nutty. Routinely the daily copy of sportswriters bristled with colorful comments that collectively and individually identified nuts.

Among the great sportswriters' sallies the late Red Smith's are especially treasured by his fans. Because Smith believed that a writer's tongue should ever repose in its natural habitat, the left cheek, he never failed his readers. As a nut designator Smith could call Bowie Kuhn "the greatest commissioner since Spike Eckert" and with barbed sarcasm could pronounce the "free agent system ... the greatest thing to happen to baseball since Candy Cummings invented the curve."

It would take volumes to exhaust the witticisms and witlesscisms of the media people. And along the way one would bump into deliriously nutty statisticians, dubbed "figure filberts" by one quipster. The original might have been Ernie Lanigan, a notorious flake who daily amazed historian Lee Allen by routinely ordering a breakfast of ham and eggs with a shot of whiskey. Usually he left the ham and eggs.

E. The Fans

Any review of baseball's nutty characters must include the fans, that wellspring from which all other constituencies of the game arise. Like the term "kranks" which it replaced, the word "fans" in the minds of many is synonymous with nuts. Ubiquitous fans crop up as collectivities and as individuals. Collectivities include the ballpark crowds, the newspaper fans, radio and TV fans, and the collectors and fetish freaks. Among the latter sort, some now shell out big money to players for autographs. One collector freak paid $25,000 for a 1910 Honus Wagner card.

As for the ballpark fans, their ranks have always shown madcap tendencies. The victorious pennant celebrations of fans have often been riotous; victory-sated fans tear up playing fields and sometimes trash cities as happened during the Big Buc Binge of 1970 and the Tigers' 1984 victory. Other notorious riots include that Cleveland Beer Riot of 1974 and Chicago's Disco Riot of 1979.

But in the annals of nutty ballpark fans it is the individual characters who stand out. Still remembered fondly in Brooklyn is Hilda Chester and her jangling cowbell and barbaric yawp; on one occasion she dispatched a note to manager Durocher telling him to pull his starting pitcher, and Durocher, thinking the note came from his boss, actually did. Another notorious individual was the curvaceous stripper, Morganna the Wild One, who on several occasions sallied onto the field at Cincinnati and elsewhere and confronted on-deck batters with her resistless demand of "kiss me."

Certainly baseball's penchant for inspiring tomfoolery and laughter goes far in helping to explain the game's mythic hold on the American populace. This is a point that major league promoters ought never to forget. When cursing hefty salaries or thanking the god Mammon for hefty TV contracts, such worthies should take time to breathe another prayer, "Thank God for nuts."

AN ALL-NUT TEAM FROM MAJOR LEAGUE BASEBALL

Pitchers — Bugs Raymond, Pascual Perez, Bo Belinsky, Lefty Gomez, Dizzy and Daffy Dean, and relievers Al Hrabosky and Moe Drabowsky.

Catchers — Yogi Berra, Clyde Kluttz and Earl Battey.

Infielders — Fred Merkle, Dick Stuart, Ed Bouchee, 1b; Billy Martin, 2b; Garry Templeton, ss; and Germany Schaefer, 3b.

Outfielders — Jim Piersall, Frenchy Bordagaray, Dizzy Nutter, Leon "Daddywags" Wagner, Babe Herman and Peanuts Lowrey.

Owners — Bill Veeck, Charley Finley, Chris von der Ahe, George Steinbrenner and Judge Emil Fuchs (consortium).

Manager — Casey Stengel.

Groundskeeper — Maury Wills.

Commissioner — Spike Eckert.

Chief Scout — Leon (John Dillinger) Hamilton.

Team Talisman — Charles "Victory" Faust.

Baseball and the Life of the Mind

By JOHN HILDEBIDLE

YEARS AGO, in a more contentious time, a few friends and I compiled a catalog of choices, guaranteed to provoke controversy within any group of bright young minds in which we happened to find ourselves. The list has, blessedly, been lost; its flavor may be suggested by one of the few items I can recall: Oreo cookies vs. Hydrox. It may be that the whole thing worked because we were then so attuned to confrontation; but I've tested it at a later time, and it still worked. From such minute passions much of life is built; my four-year-old son, out of what depths of error I can't begin to imagine, already insists on Hydrox. One item on that old list was baseball. Half the room would grow electric with reminiscence and debate, alive with names: Mantle, Spahn, Seaver, Clemente. The other half would at first purse their lips in bored disapproval; but before long they too would grow passionate, in defense of the pointlessness, the boredom, the irrelevancy ("relevant" being the prime buzz-word back then) of the Great American Game.

I was delighted, in opening Donald Hall's collection *Fathers Playing Catch With Sons: Essays on Sport [Mostly Baseball]* (North Point Press), to find that he shares my experience: "Half of my poet-friends think I am insane to waste my time writing about sports... The other half would murder to take my place." That baseball, of all sports, is a game with a particular fascination, not just for poets, but for intellectuals generally, can be verified by a rough list of the names Hall finds good reason to mention: from Whitman to Gregory Corso, from Williams and Marianne Moore to Joel Oppenheimer, from Jane Austen (!) to John Fowles, Roth, Updike, Malamud, from H.L. Mencken to John Crowe Ransom, William Empson, and L.C. Knights, from Jack Kerouac to Mark Harris to a distinguished president of Yale. One might add more—, John Cheever, if I remember correctly, once offered some observations on novelists as Yankee fans; the distinguished classicist Emily Vermeule could not resist occupying the pages of *The Boston Globe* every so often to link Sophocles and Carl Yastrzemski.

To the premise that the game of phenoms, flaky southpaws, "velocity" and "location" and "stuff" and Texas-leaguers and "heat" and "cheese" and screwballs is somehow also the game of those whose home field is their own brain, I would add one more, far more debatable, notion: that long after the last chilly moment of the World Series (the clever folk who run the major leagues apparently have never read Keats and fail to realize that baseball is, like autumn, the close bosom-friend of the maturing sun; so they play games in the dark of night in places like Detroit), much too long before the first rosy glow of spring training, when everyone's a contender—in the midst of a New England winter is the perfect time to read through a stack of volumes devoted to baseball. Mr. Hall wisely remarks that no one ever converted someone to a love of any sport by writing a book about it; sports books are always sermons to the already converted. But I think I may at least be able to account for the second of my notions, which depends in its turn upon yet another premise: that the excitement of baseball lies not in what occurs on the field (baseball-haters belabor the point that for much of the time *nothing* happens on the field: true, but what does it matter?), but in the forces of memory and imagination.

Donald Hall traces the roots of his own passion for the game back to his own youthful incompetence (which, in his forties, he was able to prove in the heat of combat, at a Pittsburgh Pirates training camp) and a father who was a pretty good shortstop, good enough to get a nibble from a double-A team. From that he generalizes the case:

> Baseball is fathers and sons . . . Baseball is the generations, looping backward forever with a million apparitions of sticks and balls, cricket and rounders, and the games the Iroquois played in Connecticut before the English came. Baseball is fathers and sons playing catch, lazy and murderous, wild and controlled, the profound archaic song of birth, growing, age and death. This diamond encloses what we are.

Taken in isolation, these few lines are a case in point of the intellectual manipulation of baseball—a reduction to the personal coupled with an expansion to the cosmic. This is Mr. Hall in his baseball-as-pastoral guise, or as he puts it, with due irony, in the title of a graceful short essay, his elaboration of "Baseball and the Meaning of Life," an enterprise in which he admits borrowing from John Crowe Ransom. But he has other hats, as when he calmly pronounces that "Baseball sets off the meaning of life precisely because it is pure of meaning." One awaits the echo of that supremely useful remark of Whitman's: "Do I contradict myself? Very well I contradict myself . . ." But *argue* would suit the case better than *contradict*; Hall's book, like all good baseball talk, is full of argument, and especially of that argument which is essential to an appreciation of the game, the inescapable yet enlivening discord between fact (a group of not-especially-interesting, highly over-specialized, largely childish and flabby men playing a game which is repetitious and slow-paced) and myth (what Hall compellingly calls "The Country of Baseball," a land in which Joe DiMaggio endlessly glides back toward a fly ball). The intersection of the two can be odd in the extreme—Hall's fathers and sons, for instance, unexpectedly bumping into the ghosts of the Iroquois; or the moment at the heart of a poem that Hall includes in his book, which watches the aged, fat, slow, clumsy figure of Ted Williams lumber after a fly ball, in the company of Achilles.

It would be a mistake, however, to confuse passion (which informs this kind of mythography, and all baseball arguments) with seriousness of any true sort. One can argue baseball at the dinner table without fear of disinheritance. Even those arch enemies, player and umpire, turn out to be able to chat amiably about this and that before the game, as Hall watches them do, only to spew vituperation at one another a few minutes later over the precise trajectory of a ball thrown faster than the human eye can accurately register. So too at each moment of the game there is time for an expenditure of tremendous mental energy—an energy of reflection, judgment, reconsideration, and inevitably of argument. Baseball is the only sport in which this kind of meditative attention is built in (what else is there to do between pitches?) and in which the fundamental acts are clear, distinct, slow, and individual enough to allow anyone to feel confident in judging. Each football play is an elaborate interaction of at least twenty-three parts, players and ball; no one can adequately assess them all, even with a few replays, which is why football coaches and players obsessively re-view each filmed moment. Basketball is just too fast, and so is hockey; they are games of amazement and emotion, not of analysis.

This is one reason why baseball indulges itself so luxuriantly in numbers, the ultimate symbolization of "fact," the most seemingly firm (but actually suppositious) basis of argumentative opinion. One striking fact about Hall's book is the degree to which he skips the numbers; my own experience is that it's impossible to talk baseball for more than five minutes without swimming in ERAs, on-base percentages, and the like—all twisted from their true, descriptive nature to become prognostications about the next pitch, the next home-stand, the next season. The full glory of this sort of thing can be tasted in any volume of *The Bill James Baseball Abstract*, once mimeographed, later published every spring, each edition a masterpiece of polemical statistics, of dream and prejudice gussied up with algebra. Read in March, the book will prepare you to hold your own in the bleachers at Fenway; read in January, after the season has made a hash of so many of the firm predictions of James and his co-religionists (they have named themselves *saber-maticians*), the book is a lesson in the vanity of human imaginings. Read what James had to say one spring about Dave Kingman; and then consider what the enigmatic Mr. Kingman, against all probabilities, accomplished during the season itself.

This proliferation of data is not only the raw matter of argument; it is as well a keystone in the pseudo-scholarship of the sport—that body of lore which helps the baseball fan compound his or her imagining of what is about to happen. There are in fact two kinds of baseball lore, one of which can be acquired early (as soon as one's arithmetical talents have progressed to long division) and in private, the other built up slowly by watching, talking, listening, reading. The first is number and its cousin, trivia (who threw the pitch Babe Ruth hit for his last homer?); it is scholarship without the awful burdens of relevance. The second is something more like folk tale or legend, the communal memory of games seen, passed on from one generation to the next, provoked most richly by a chain of association with some passing moment in the game actually in progress: "A hit? Forget it, it's an error all the way. Now Marty Marion, he'd have gotten to that one in his sleep. I remember a game with the Browns, late innings, and this guy, I forget his name but he played with Pittsburgh later, left-handed, anyway he gets fooled on the pitch and tops the ball to shortstop, and Marty . . ."

This train of lore is an endless stock of image and narrative: the pattern of a long-dead pitcher's motion, the day (this is one of Hall's best yarns) Dock Ellis hit the first four Reds he pitched to, and on purpose. It seems to demand an expenditure of memory, almost a kind of pedantry, which is no small charm for those whose work is real pedantry; but in fact it can just as easily be fueled by imagination pretending to recall: the way it must have been, the event replayed, re-shot from just the perfect angle, with the balance of surprise and expectation to be found in listening yet once more to a well-loved symphony.

Or to put it more directly: Those of us headed, ultimately, for some sort of life-long brainwork begin, early on, to sense the power of knowing something (anything!), the delight of forming it imaginatively, of judging and then spinning out the reasons. And those skills can without pain or censure—or much difficulty—be exercised while reclining in a dark bedroom, armed with a flashlight, a pencil-stub, and a scorebook, next to a radio at lowest volume tuned to a night game from somewhere out West. With luck, and if your eyes aren't too hollow in the morning, it will take years for your mother to catch on.

I seem to have followed Mr. Hall in circling back to childhood: which is fair enough, since it's hard to imagine anyone becoming a baseball fan in middle age. I hesitate to introduce the subject of children's games, which are nowadays over-studied; it can't be long until we have an MLA Division of Play Studies (Ludology?). But there are at least two ways in which baseball is especially congenial to the play of children: the ease of imitating the game, and its peculiar interrelationship of individual and group. Shocken Books issued a collection called *New York Street Games and Other Stories and Sketches,* by Meyer Liben. It is mostly a memorial to Liben, who died (as George Dennison's long and warm foreword informs us) in 1975 after a life of serious but largely unrecognized writing. Mr. Dennison makes brave claims for the book ("the ongoing, comprehensive anthology of important American work, that exists both in our affections and our judgment, would be radically incomplete without examples of the fiction of Meyer Liben")—claims for which "judgment" would find it hard to discover more than one or two supporting examples among the pieces collected here. But for the sports nut, the first third of the book, a series of fictions/reminiscences of street games of the 1930's, has an inescapable appeal.

The particular sports which enter are sometimes surprising. There is, for example, a fine understated piece concerned with a Rabbi who tries to understand why the boy whom he is training for a Bar Mitzvah ignores Hebrew in favor of practicing to win the hop-step-and-jump at some future Olympic Games. What is unmistakable is the degree to which these children are remaking the world of adulthood. This has, by now, become a cliche of child psychology; but no cliche should make us ignore the power of this kind of creative imitation. Liben catches it best in the story of Davey Flaxman, whose hero, the boxer Benny Leonard, has just—inconceivably—lost his title. Davey's victory over an older tough eccentrically known as The Gate is an effort to restore some justice to the world, with mixed but, in the short term at least, largely positive results. Davey's sister is shocked by the damage Davey's face has suffered; we—and Davey too—can imagine what his parents will have to say; but Davey, falling into a satisfied sleep, "exulted, having fought in the manner of his peerless champion, and for his vindication."

Now this sort of imitation, as Liben's examples show, can be lavished on any sport, and I might as well acknowledge here the number of children at this moment imagining themselves to be Walter Payton or Carl Lewis or Martina Navratilova or Michael Jordan. But it also must be said that no child can long ignore the peculiarity of most professional athletes, a peculiarity which, like Wallace Stevens's perfect poem, resists the most powerful imaginative intelligence. Football players are, after all, mammoth, and far too tolerant of the agony of collision; hockey players dash around an enclosed space full of knife blades, sticks, and flying objects, with a bravery rather too close to self-destructive madness; basketball players possess a height and grace and physical intelligence which no dream can quite capture. Baseball players, by contrast, are shockingly normal-looking. There are eleven year olds taller than Freddy Patek and more muscular than Bruce Kison. Many players (and especially pitchers) are gangly, eccentrically built, and thus much like children, whose proportions are, by adult standards, invariably wrong; others are flabby and slow. The salvation of my overweight early adolescence was the accomplishment of Smokey Burgess, the plumpest and yet the finest pinch-hitter I ever saw. One can quite readily imagine oneself not as good as, but even better than, one's hero. And what these mortals do takes so little equipment, no mast or net or racket; just an easily portable ball. Or less than that: You can quite adequately replay the World Series using apples thrown at a stone wall or rocks thrown at a dumpster with a strike-zone chalked on its side.

It seems so easy: just touch a ball with a stick, just throw the ball from here to there, or catch it. A four year old can catch, for Pete's sake. And if you can't hit worth a damn, if a thrown or rolling ball inspires only fear and incompetence in your heart, you can specialize in the two absolutely risk-free baseball skills: the wiggles between pitches (want to see me do check-my-cup? Or spit? Or do Rocky-Colavito-in-the-on-deck-circle?); and bench-jockeying, which demands only a loud voice and a certain taste for alliterative rhythm: "Hey, hey, hey, how you hum-baby!"

I'm not sure it's necessarily the case that writers and intellectuals are clumsier children than the average; but I wouldn't be surprised. I was, and Donald Hall unashamedly admits he was, and William Carlos Williams had this funny heart condition they said meant he shouldn't exert himself. In any case it is beyond question that they spend too much time—by the world's standards—thinking, watching, daydreaming; which leaves less time for perfecting your hook shot or your lob (although Galway Kinnell seems to have managed that, somehow), and which increases the likelihood you'll be looking for a sport which minimizes accomplishment and maximizes observation and charade. Simply in terms of time, baseball is it. I spent a few hours one summer watching the Red Sox play the Indians on TV, armed with a couple of stopwatches. By my rough calculation, not counting the time between innings, and counting each pitch (no matter how errant) as an action, five-sixths of each inning was devoted to the space between events. If you put your mind to it, you could probably write *Moby Dick* at Shea Stadium and never miss a single out.

Liben puts his finger on one other element of street games. Here is the central moment in a game (and a story) called "Lady, I Did It," the basic action of which is the ringing of random doorbells:

> . . . we chose one among us to step forward
> and commit, for all of us, the predetermined
> act.

> He stepped forward swiftly, with a courage partly determined by the presence of the rest of us, partly by the role toward which he advanced, and partly by the ordinary amount of the spirit of play which he possessed, and pushed the button. He stepped back into the anonymity of the group and we closed ranks about him, as a protective cover, until the moment when he would step forward and expose himself as the culprit.

The key here is the fluidity with which each player moves from group to individual, and back again: from star to audience, from darer to supporter—a fluidity which retains, however, a great deal of self-control. The group may choose the "culprit" (although you can be certain that principles of justice will be enforced; and that litigation may always be used to avoid the responsibilities of election) but once chosen the individual determines precisely his distance from the group, retaining his allegiance both to himself and to others.

By comparison, here is C.I.R. James talking, in a chapter called "What Is Art?" in his *Beyond a Boundary*. He is speaking of that baffling (to Americans) game, cricket:

> It is so organized that at all times it is compelled to reproduce the central action which characterizes all good drama from the days of the Greeks to our own: two individuals pitted against each other in a conflict that is strictly personal but no less strictly representative of a social group . . . Even the baseball-batter, who most nearly approaches this particular aspect of cricket, may and often does find himself after a fine hit standing on one of the bases, where he is now dependent upon others. The batsman

> facing the ball does not merely represent his side. For that moment, for all intents and purposes, he is his side. This fundamental relation of the One and the Many, Individual and Social, Individual and Universal, leader and followers, representative and ranks, the part and the whole, is structurally imposed on the players of cricket. What other sports, games, and arts have to aim at, the players are given to start with, they cannot depart from it.

Mr. James's dismissal of baseball is a part of the interminable war between fans of the two games; about which books by the score remain to be written, the best of all written by someone with a particular kind of bilingualism which is beyond me, someone equally at home with knuckleball pitchers and slow-bowlers, cutoff-men and silly mid-off. But the important point here is the enlargement, into the "adult" world of cricket, of the fluid relation at the heart of "Lady, I Did It."

What, to Mr. James, is a fault of baseball, in terms of pure drama, is—I would argue—a great advantage, especially to the child and the thinker. Those baserunners are not so dependent as Mr. James says. There are things to be done: stealing, taking the extra base, just dancing and diddling around enough to catch the pitcher's eye and ruin his concentration. In those small ways the chorus can enter the drama. And there is the opportunity to pass on the responsibility ("just get on base and let Mickey hit one out . . ."), which is a great reassurance to the faint-of-heart and the slow-of-hand. To take such an easy way out gives one the best seat in the house, close enough to feel engaged in the fundamental conflict, to excite the mind into prediction; far enough not to have to worry overmuch about blame. And, finally, to this universal *agon* baseball adds the charitable element of sacrifice—the bunt, hitting behind the runner, even just swinging so mightily (if inaccurately) as to scare off the catcher and let the stealing runner be safe. There is a whole world, in baseball, just at the edge of the spotlight, where the supporting shadows are comfortingly near.

James's book is full of clever argument, and of a music I can only hear, without the faintest idea of the sense behind it. What on earth *is* a googly? I've been told, again and again, but I can't remember. What is, however, electric about the book, even to an obtuse American, is the richness of interpretation of which I've given only a taste: Here is the imaginative (and, in this case, highly political) mind at work on a "mere" game. The child imitates and imagines, takes the hero's part and then rushes back to the open arms of the gang; to which pleasure the "adult" mind adds that of interpretation. Even in the more youthful work of Liben's games, that kind of decoding intelligence enters in, comically, as the older boys (doing their own kind of imitation of the adult) observe their brothers. So teen-age Jerry watches a game of King of the Hill:

> Jerry was a Freudian, and he thought, watching the game, that here was another illustration of the theory of the Primal Horde . . . Jerry was also a Marxist (it was before the time of the Freudo-Marxists) and he saw this game as another illustration of the endless struggle for power that was going on everywhere . . .

It is all too short a step from there to the ponderous solemnity of academic analysis of sport; but no longer a step to Hall or to James, who are anything but ponderous. The only difference is the providential force of good sense.

Of course nowadays everything can be, and must be, decoded; otherwise how could Roland Barthes hold up his head in intellectual company after writing about wrestling? I quoted a while back Donald Hall's paradoxical formulation—that what makes baseball meaningful is its lack of meaning, if I may paraphrase this time. There is so much about the game which teases the mind into a search for meaning—the basic simplicity of the game itself, within a complex veil of proliferating rules, which once produced a *Saturday Evening Post* series called "So You Think You Know Baseball," which for years provoked the nearest thing to intellectual conversation in my neighborhood. Or all those mystic numbers, three, seven, nine. Or the history of the game, full of social class (it began as the Gentleman's Game), money, race, scandal—all of which can be considered at your leisure by way of David Quentin Voigt's three ample, judicious, and loving volumes on *American Baseball* (Penn State University Press). Or simply the attention which is paid to the game, the human aspiration, effort, and exasperation it summons forth; surely this all must signify *something*.

What is more likely is that baseball, like Ahab's doubloon, signifies everything; that it calls up what Philip Larkin has called, in a poem about jazz, "appropriate falsehood" in each observing eye. Baseball, to dabble in jargon, is a set of undetermined signs; a situation which no intellectual can long resist. Even the doubters can be entrapped, by way of their effort to elaborate the lunacies of fanhood as yet another Chilling Commentary on the State of Modern Culture. The cleverest among us—my teeth at this point grind in envy of Donald Hall for his deft four pages on the subject—manage to have it both ways, to see meaning and meaninglessness at the same time, thus accomplishing the Keatsian trick of "being in uncertainties without any irritable reaching after fact and reason" (Keats would unquestionably have been a fan of the Cubs and of relief-pitching). Baseball is, looked at this way, the great and addictive escape of the interpretive mind—an escape which allows the interpretive muscles to stay in shape.

As Robert Coover insists at the very end of his finely-crafted puzzle of a novel, *The Universal Baseball Association, Inc.* (Signet/NAL), "It's not a trial. It's not even a lesson. It's just what it is." Of course Coover supplies this moral to a book which investigates the mind of a man who "found his way back to baseball. Nothing like it really. Not the actual game so much—to tell the truth, real baseball bored him—but rather the records, the statistics, the peculiar balances between individual and team, offense and defense, strategy and luck, accident and pattern, power and intelligence." Coover slyly balances metaphysics and actualities; his hero is a rather derelict accountant, J. Henry Waugh—who is also, and not altogether ironically, Yahweh.

Coover's accomplishment—and what is, to my eye, the failure of Philip Roth and Bernard Malamud, both of whom have also toyed with baseball and the meaning of life—suggests one general rule about baseball writing: Outside is better than Inside. That is to say, the best writing comes not from an effort to understand the game itself so much as an effort to capture and record what occurs in the minds of the onlookers, because it is there that imagination is at work. A few years ago the comic strip *Shoe* had Cosmo Fishhawk, journalist, thinker, and fan, take the cynical Shoe to the ballpark, insisting, "It's really an intellectual game." To which replies Shoe, sarcastically but accurately, "The only action is going on in the minds of the spectators."

In baseball as among the intelligentsia, there is always more to be said—about the peculiar centrality of failure to the game (the best hitters flop seven out of ten times; the most loved teams are often hopelessly second-best); about baseball language, and especially sports writing and metaphor; about baseball's capacity to encompass change without appearing to change. On many of these points Mr. Hall speaks well and gracefully. But I think he's got one thing wrong, a sign of which is in his title and in the little prose-lyric I quoted earlier: "Baseball is fathers and sons." Even if you make that "Baseball *was* fathers and sons," in honor of all the live young female arms out there in the current country of baseball, it won't wash. It leaves out the Other Babe, nee Didrikson, who at times barnstormed, striking out eager young men, among them my father. It leaves out Hall's own wife, Jane Kenyon (a poet, of course!), who is, as he admits, as much a fan as he is; it leaves out a woman of great years and wisdom, whose name I can't recall but whose obituary in *The Boston Globe* ran under a headline which announced the determining fact of her life: BASEBALL FAN.

And it leaves out Linda Kittell, about whom Roger Angell

writes in *Late Innings* (Ballantine). In a piece called "In the Country," Angell tells how Linda, at a tender age, was in love with Whitey Ford; as a grown woman (have you guessed that she's a poet too?), her idea of a romantic weekend is an overnight drive to Seattle to see the Mariners and Yanks in the Kingdome. About Roger Angell only one kind of argument is possible; you must concede that he is incomparably the best writer-about-baseball we have, and probably ever have had. But you can propose your own favorite from among his pieces, collected and current. "The Web of the Game" (Smokey Joe Wood, erstwhile conqueror of the Big Train, Walter Johnson himself, watches Ron Darling pitch a no-hitter in a key college game at Yale, and lose) is what the sports writers call a consensus choice, although any time Angell looks at Tom Seaver or one of the Red Sox near-misses something magic happens, and he can write ten riveting pages on "The Ball," and there's one on Bob Gibson that proves how essential a kind of focused malice is to baseball success (Ty Cobb, my friends, was not a nice person), and one on catching and another, farther back, on Steve Blass, who lost it overnight.

But the best of them all, especially if you don't believe that baseball has anything to do with life as it is ordinarily lived, is "In the Country," which never goes near a major-league ballpark or an agent or a winning team, but which is nevertheless a love story: Linda's love for an aging southpaw who dropped out of baseball (for good reasons) but came back; Angell's affection for her and him; and the love of all three for baseball, a love uncomplicated by analysis (there are any number of facts much, much more important than any meaning we give them), but inextricably tied to human aspiration, to that sense of growing old which strikes absurdly early, to emotion and good sense for once not quite at war with one another.

So what you should do is stay home and read. As the snow falls and while somewhere, no matter how chill the air, some small body is trying to make a snowball break down and away, read Bill James and pretend to bring order out of chaos, to know how the future grows from the past; read David Quentin Voigt and pretend to be a scholar; read Roger Angell and encounter the ever-rich quotidian; read *The Universal Baseball Association* and play both God and cynic; read Donald Hall (who will, if you are at all susceptible, tell you what else to read, both verse and "Prose-ball") and dream—of Peewee Reese taking Carl Hubbell deep; of Ted Williams's perfect swing and even more perfect arrogance; of one more flirtation with .400 by Wade Boggs or someone we don't know yet, who (given the state of the world) is learning, like the doomed Sandinista Oriole fan in the film *Under Fire*, to read the rotation on a slider by watching the trajectory of a hand-grenade; of Ryne Sandberg whirling past second base (maybe he even touched the bag) and throwing over to Bull Durham *in* time for the out, a double-dip and the Cards strand the go-ahead run: Dream of the long summer afternoon which is truly endless. "The business of baseball," the wise Mr. Hall observes, "like the business of art is dream"—to which I must add that, when it comes to baseball, the dreams are, happily, those from which no responsibility is ever born.

The Editor

Peter C. Bjarkman *(a.k.a. "Doctor Baseball") is a free-lance author and editor who has written more than a dozen baseball books, ranging from encyclopedic reference works to anthologies, coffee table histories and juvenile biographies. A resident of Lafayette, Indiana, he once taught linguistics and literature at Purdue University, before discovering that pennant races are more titillating than tenure tracks, and that the air is still far purer in the bleachers at Wrigley Field than anywhere within the academic ivy tower.*

Author's Roster

Stephen Jay Gould (*1st Base*) is an accomplished natural historian who teaches biology, geology, and the history of science at Harvard University. He also ranks high among the most insightful intellectual commentators on the subtleties of our nation's favored pastime. Like most academics who have been inspired to write on baseball, Professor Gould was once amused to find that his early pontifications on the national game generated far more citation than all his scientific works.

Mark Harris (*Shortstop*) is author of fifteen novels and creator of the beloved Henry Wiggens' tetrology of baseball fictions—*The Southpaw*, *Bang the Drum Slowly*, *A Ticket for Seamstitch*, and *It Looked Like Forever*. Also a teacher of creative writing at Arizona State University, Mr. Harris may properly be reckoned the spiritual father of the serious adult baseball novel.

Jay Feldman (*Outfield*) writes prolifically about baseball (for *Sports Illustrated* and other popular magazines), has organized annual "Baseball for Peace" ballplaying tours to Nicaragua, and plays in an over-30 hardball league in California. If he still can't hit the curve ball, Jay certainly can spin a wicked essay about the national pastime.

John S. Bowman (*Designated Hitter*) is a prolific author of scholarly and coffee table volumes, covering topics as diverse as baseball history, the Civil War, American furniture and European travel. Native to Massachusetts and a current resident of Northampton, he has enjoyed a distinguished editorial and literary career, yet still counts as his proudest moment an appearance on local television news while catching practice pitches for his Little League son.

Bill Fitsell (*3rd Base*) professes origins as mysterious as the mythical Casey of Mudville himself, but such murky heritage does not belie his ability to dismantle one of baseball's most cherished literary myths. Regular contributor to the "People" column for the Kingston (Ontario) *Whig-Standard Magazine*, Fitzell is a dedicated sports enthusiast and an amateur historian of some accomplishment.

James Kissane (*Outfield*) currently teaches American letters and literature in the Department of English at Grinnell College in Iowa. He wasted away his formative years in unrestrained glory, however, playing catch in Pocatello, Idaho.

Thomas L. Altherr (*Outfield*) is professor of history and American Studies at Metropolitan State College in Denver, holds a Ph.D. in history from Ohio State University, and takes impish delight in highlighting lesser-known facts about the persistence of our national pastime in the formation and sustenance of the collective American imagination.

Dave Healy (*RHP*) and **Paul Healy** (*LHP*) are not—contrary to some recent circulating rumors—merely surreptitious pseudonyms for Jim Lemon and Harmon Killebrew. Yet these two residents of the Twin Cities area have contributed nearly as much with their perspicacious essays in the *Minneapolis Review of Baseball* to Minnesota baseball lore as have the aforementioned pair of erstwhile sluggers.

John B. Holway (*Utility*) is perhaps the nation's leading historian of Negro League baseball and author of five books on black ballplayers, including his *Blackball Stars* which earned a 1989 Casey Award as best baseball book of the year. He lives in suburban Washington, D.C., where he recently retired from governmental service to devote full-time energies to writing about our national pastime and other vitally American topics.

Merritt Clifton (*Relief Pitcher*) is a long-time environmental advocate who has built a solid reputation, as well, as a talented purveyor of underground baseball literature. Founder of Samisdat Press in Vermont, he has produced the landmark small press novella *A Baseball Classic* (1978) and numerous other engaging stories and essays.

William Humber (*2nd Base*) is premier baseball historian in the neighboring nation of Canada. A coordinator of Continuing Education courses at Toronto's Seneca College and organizer of a popular winter-time "Hot Stove League" baseball culture course, he is perhaps best known as author of a volume entitled *Cheering for the Home Team: The Story of Baseball in Canada* (1983).

David Q. Voigt (*Coach*) was as instrumental in lending legitimacy to the serious authorship of baseball history as was Mark Harris in providing similar status for the adult baseball novel. Author of a praised three-volume pioneering history of the game, he maintains a position as one of the game's most valuable scholarly chroniclers. He is also professor of sociology at Albright College in Pennsylvania.

John Hildebidle (*Manager*) is still to be found—as he was when he contributed to our earlier fiction companion volume—in the academic big leagues, teaching writing and literature at MIT. As all who live in the shadows of Fenway Park, he is an ordained expert on the more heroic and melancholy elements of baseball history.

Acknowledgments

Selections in this volume by Peter C. Bjarkman, John S. Bowman, Merritt Clifton and William Humber are appearing here in print for the first time. The following previously published essays appear with generous permission of their original publishers and/or authors, to whom we are greatly indebted.

"Why No One Hits .400 Any More" (Stephen Jay Gould) from *Discover* (August 1986): 60-66. Reprinted with the permission of *Discover* and the author.

"Horatio at the Bat, or Why Such a Lengthy Embryonic Period for the Serious Baseball Novel?" (Mark Harris) from *Aethlon: The Journal of Sport Literature* 5:2 (Spring 1988): 1-11. Reprinted with permission of *Aethlon*, the author, and his agent.

"Little League: An Idea Whose Time Has Come ... And Gone" (Jay Feldman) from *Newsweek* (May 22, 1989): 8. Reprinted with permission from *Newsweek* and the author.

"Was Casey a Canuck?" (Bill Fitsell) from *The Whig-Standard Magazine* (October 8, 1985): 5-7. Reprinted with permission of the author.

"Baseball and the Urban Crisis" (James Kissane) from *The Grinnell Magazine* (September-October 1969): 16-18. Reprinted with the permission of Grinnell College and the author.

"The New Mythopoeism of Baseball: W.P. Kinsella's Baseball Fiction" (Thomas L. Altherr) from *Minneapolis Review of Baseball* 10:2 (1991): 23-32. A revised version also appeared under the same title in *Cooperstown: Symposium on Baseball and the American Culture* (1990), published by Meckler Books. Reprinted with permission of Meckler Corporation, MRB (Brown-Benchmark Publishers), and the author.

"Half-Cultivated Fields: Symbolic Landscapes of Baseball" (Dave Healy and Paul Healy) from *Minneapolis Review of Baseball* 8:3 (1989): 31-37, 64. Reprinted with permission of MRB (Brown-Benchmark Publishers), and the authors.

"Diamond Stars: Baseball Astrology" (John B. Holway) from *The National Pastime* 6 (Winter 1987): 56-61. Reprinted with permission of the Society for American Baseball Research (SABR) and the authors.

"Thank God for Nuts! They Flavor the Game" (David Q. Voigt) from *Baseball Research Journal* 14 (1985): 46-51. Reprinted with permission of the Society for American Baseball Research (SABR) and the author.

"Baseball and the Life of the Mind" (John Hildebidle) from *New England Review and Bread Loaf Quarterly* 7:2 (Winter 1984): 252-264. Reprinted with permission of *New England Review* and the author.

The editor is also indebted to the following for their special assistance and favors: Birch Brook Press publisher Tom Tolnay for his continued faith in the project; my unofficial agents Ronnie Wilbur and John Bowman, for a thousand and one things; and Bill Friday, for finding all those neat things to read in the off-season.

All-Star Essays & Articles for the Serious Fan

Baldassaro, Lawrence. "Ted Williams: The Reluctant Hero" in: *Journal of American Culture* 4:3 (Fall 1981) 66-74.

Berlange, Gai Ingham. "Five Forgotten Women in American Baseball History: Players, Lizzie Arlington, Alta Weiss, Lizzie Murphy; Umpire, Amanda Clement; and Owner, Helen Britton" in: *Cooperstown Symposium on Baseball and the American Culture, 1990.* Westport, Connecticut: Meckler Books, 1991, 222-242.

Bick, Mario. "Double Play: Notes on American Baseball" in: *Annals of the New York Academy of Sciences: Papers in Anthropology and Linguistics,* Edited by May C. Ebihara and Rosamond Gianutsos. Volume 318 (1978), 37-49.

Bjarkman, Peter C. "Six-Pointed Diamonds and the Ultimate Shiksa: Baseball and the American-Jewish Immigrant Experience" in: *Cooperstown Symposium on Baseball and the American Culture, 1990.* Westport, Connecticut: Meckler Books, 1991, 306-347.

Bluthardt, Robert F. "Fenway Park and the Golden Age of the Baseball Park" in: *Journal of Popular Culture* 21:1 (Summer 1987), 43-52.

Boswell, Thomas. "99 Reasons Why Baseball is Better than Football" in: *The Heart of the Order.* New York: Doubleday and Company, 1989, 29-37.

Bouchier, Nancy and Robert Knight Barney. "A Critical Examination of a Source on Early Ontario Baseball: The Reminiscence of Adam E. Ford" in: *Journal of Sports History* 15:1 (Spring 1988), 75-90.

Clifton, Merritt. "Where the Twain Shall Meet: What Baseball Means to Japan and Humanity" in: *The National Pastime: A Review of Baseball History* 4 (1985), 12-22.

Crepeau, Richard C. "Pearl Harbor: A Failure of Baseball?" in: *Journal of Popular Culture* 15:4 (Spring 1982), 67-74.

Folsom, Ed. "The Manly and Healthy Game: Walt Whitman and the Development of American Baseball" in: *Arete: The Journal of Sport Literature* 2:1 (1984), 43-62.

Garrett, Roland. "The Metaphysics of Baseball" in: *Philosophy Today* 20 (1976), 209-225.

Gelber, Steven M. "Working at Playing: The Culture of the Workplace and Rise of Baseball" in: *Journal of Social History* 16 (Summer 1983), 3-22.

Giamatti, A. Bartlett. "Baseball and the American Character" in: *Harper's Magazine* 273 (October 1986), 27-30.

Gould, Stephen Jay. "The Creation Myths of Cooperstown" in: *Natural History* (November 1989), 14-24.

Gould, Stephen Jay. "Winning and Losing: Its All in the Game" in: *Rotunda* 21 (Spring 1989), 25-31.

Grella, George. "Baseball and the American Dream" in: *Massachusetts Review* 16:3 (Summer 1975), 550-567.

Grossinger, Richard. "Baseball During the Middle Ages" in: *Baseball I Gave You the Best Years of My Life.* Edited by Kevin Kerrane and Richard Grossinger. Richmond, California: North Atlantic Books, 1980, 348-351.

Harris, Mark. "Maybe What Baseball Needs Is a Henry David Thoreau" in: *Short Work of It: Selected Writing by Mark Harris.* Pittsburgh: The University of Pittsburgh Press (1979), 120-129.

Kahn, Roger. "Intellectuals and Ballplayers" in: *American Scholar* 26 (1957), 342-349.

Lamoreaux, David. "Baseball in the Late Nineteenth Century: The Source of its Appeal" in: *Journal of Popular Culture* 11:3 (Winter 1977), 597-613.

McMartin, Jim. "The Diamond Sport—A Jung Man's Game that Appeals to All" in: *Baseball Research Journal* 13 (1984), 34-35.

Memmott, A. James. "Wordsworth in the Bleachers: The Baseball Essays of Roger Angell" in: *Journal of American Culture* 5:2 (Summer 1982), 42-51.

Nelson, Don. "A Tale of Two Sluggers: Roger Maris and Hack Wilson" in: *The National Pastime: A Review of Baseball History* 1 (1982), 32-33.

Oriard, Michael V. "Sports & Space" in: *Baseball I Gave You the Best Years of My Life.* Edited by Kevin Kerrane and Richard Grossinger. Richmond, California: North Atlantic Books, 1980, 59-63.

Palmer, William. "History, Tradition, and Hubris: The Baseball Universe of Roger Angell" in: *Journal of Popular Culture* 20:2 (Fall 1986), 17-28.

Plasketes, George. "The Rebel Hero in Baseball: Bill Spaceman Lee in an Orbit All his Own" in: *Journal of Popular Culture* 21:1 (Summer 1987), 121-138.

Roberts, Frederic. "A Myth Grows in Brooklyn: Urban Death, Resurrection, and the Brooklyn Dodgers" in: *Baseball History* 2:2 (Summer 1987), 4-26.

Santa Maria, Michael and James Costello. "Knee-Deep in Mudville: Boneheads, Goats and Gophers" in: *Cooperstown Symposium on Baseball and the American Culture, 1990.* Westport, Connecticut: Meckler Books, 1991, 348-374.

Shattuck, Debra. "Playing a Man's Game: Women and Baseball in the United States, 1866-1954" in: *Baseball History 2.* Westport, Connecticut: Meckler Books, 1989, 57-77.

Sumner, Jim. "Tom Zachary's Perfect Season" in: *Baseball History 3.* Westport, Connecticut: Meckler Books, 1990, 89-97.

Thorn, John and Jules Tygiel. "Jackie Robinson's Signing: The Real, Untold Story" in: *The National Pastime: A Review of Baseball History* 10 (1990), 7-12.

Baseball's Fifty Essential Non-Fiction Books

Angell, Roger. *The Summer Game.* New York: The Viking Press, 1972 (New York: Ballantine Books, 1984).

Angell, Roger. *Five Seasons: A Baseball Companion.* New York: Simon and Schuster, 1977 (New York: Popular Library, 1978).

Bjarkman, Peter C. *The Baseball Scrapbook: The Men and the Magic of America's National Pastime.* New York: Dorset Press, 1991.

Boswell, Thomas. *How Life Imitates the World Series.* Garden City, New York: Doubleday and Company, 1982.

Boswell, Thomas. *Why Time Begins on Opening Day.* Garden City, New York: Doubleday and Company, 1984.

Bouton, Jim. *Ball Four: My Life and Hard Times Throwing the Knuckleball in the Big Leagues.* New York and Cleveland: The World Publishing Company, 1970.

Boyd, Brendan C. and Fred C. Harris. *The Great American Baseball Card Flipping, Trading and Bubble Gum Book.* Boston: Little, Brown and Company, 1973.

Brosnan, Jim. *The Long Season.* New York: Harper and Row, 1960 (New York: Penguin Books, 1983).

Brosnan, Jim. *Pennant Race.* New York: Harper and Row, 1962 (New York: Dell Publishing Company, 1963).

Coffin, Tristram P. *The Old Ball Game: Baseball in Folklore and Fiction.* New York: Herder and Herder Publishers, 1971.

Curran, William. *Mitts: A Celebration of the Art of Fielding.* New York: William Morrow and Company, 1985.

Einstein, Charles. *Willie's Time: A Memoir.* New York: J.P. Lippincott Company, 1979.

Fleming, G.H. *The Dizziest Season: The Gashouse Gang Chases the Pennant.* New York: William Morrow and Company, 1984.

Frommer, Harvey. *New York City Baseball: The Last Golden Age: 1947-1957.* New York: Macmillan and Company, 1980.

Gammons, Peter. *Beyond the Sixth Game: What's Happened to Baseball Since the Greatest Game in World Series History.* Boston: Houghton Mifflin Company, 1985 (Lexington, Massachusetts: The Stephen Greene Press, 1986).

Gutkind, Lee. *The Best Seat in Baseball, But You Have to Stand! (The Game as Umpires See It).* New York: Dial Press, 1975.

Halberstam, David. *Summer of '49.* New York: William Morrow and Company, 1989.

Hano, Arnold. *A Day in the Bleachers.* New York: Thomas Y. Crowell Company, 1955 (New York: Da Capo Press, 1982).

Hill, Art. *I Don't Care If I Never Come Back: A Baseball Fan and His Game.* New York: Simon and Schuster, 1980.

Honig, Donald. *Baseball When the Grass Was Real: Baseball from the Twenties to the Forties Told by the Men Who Played It.* New York: Coward, McCann and Geoghegan, 1975 (New York: Berkley Publishing, 1976).

House, Tom. *The Jocks Itch: The Fast-Track Private World of the Professional Ballplayer.* Chicago: Contemporary Books, 1989.

Humber, William. *Lets Play Ball: Inside the Perfect Game.* Toronto: Lester and Orpen Dennys, 1989.

Jordan, Pat. *A False Spring.* New York: Dodd and Mead Company, 1975 (New York: Simon and Schuster, 1988).
Kahn, James M. *The Umpire Story.* New York: G.P. Putnam's Sons, 1953.
Kahn, Roger. *The Boys of Summer.* New York: Harper and Row Publishers, 1971.
Kerrane, Kevin. *Dollar Sign on the Muscle: The World of Baseball Scouting.* New York and Toronto: Beaufort Books, 1984.
Kiernan, Thomas. *The Miracle at Coogan's Bluff.* New York: Thomas Y. Crowell Company, 1975.
Kiersh, Edward. *Where Have You Gone, Vince DiMaggio?* New York: Bantam Books, 1983.
Klein, Alan M. *Sugarball: The American Game, the Dominican Dream.* New Haven, Connecticut: Yale University Press, 1991.
Kuklick, Bruce. *To Every Thing a Season: Shibe Park and Urban Philadelphia, 1909-1976.* Princeton, New Jersey: Princeton University Press, 1991.
Lansche, Jerry. *Glory Fades Away: The Nineteenth-Century World Series Rediscovered.* Dallas, Texas: Taylor Publishing Company, 1991.
Lowenfish, Lee and Tommy Lupien. *The Imperfect Diamond: The Story of Baseball's Reserve System and the Men Who Fought to Change It.* New York: Stein and Day Publishers, 1980 (New York: Da Capo Press, 1991).
Mead, William B. *Even the Browns.* Chicago: Contemporary Books, 1978 (republished as *Baseball Goes to War,* New York: Farragut Publishing Company, 1985).
Mead, William B. *Two Spectacular Seasons (1930: The Year the Hitters Ran Wild and 1968: The Year the Pitchers Took Revenge).* New York: Macmillan Publishing Company, 1990.
Okrent, Daniel. *Nine Innings (The Anatomy of Baseball as Seen Through the Playing of a Single Game).* New York: Ticknor and Fields, 1985 (New York: McGraw-Hill, 1986).
Okrent, Daniel and Harris Lewine (Editors). *The Ultimate Baseball Book.* Boston: Houghton Mifflin Company, 1984.
Parrott, Harold. *The Lords of Baseball.* New York: Praeger Publishers, 1976.
Peary, Danny (Editor). *Cult Baseball Players: The Greats, the Flakes, the Weird and the Wonderful.* New York: Simon and Schuster, 1990.

Peterson, Robert. *Only the Ball Was White: A History of Legendary Black Players and All-Black Professional Teams.* Englewood Cliffs, New Jersey: Prentice-Hall, 1970 (New York: McGraw-Hill Book Company, 1984).

Quigley, Martin. *The Crooked Pitch: The Curveball in American Baseball History.* Chapel Hill, North Carolina: Algonquin Books, 1984.

Ritter, Lawrence S. *The Glory of Their Times: The Story of the Early Days of Baseball Told By the Men Who Played It.* New York: Collier-Macmillan, 1966.

Seidel, Michael. *Streak: Joe DiMaggio and the Summer of '41.* New York: McGraw-Hill Company, 1988 (New York: Penguin Books, 1988).

Smith, Robert. *Pioneers of Baseball.* Boston: Little, Brown and Company, 1978.

Smith, Robert. *Baseball: A Historical Narrative of the Game, the Men Who Have Played It, and Its Place in American Life.* New York: Simon and Schuster, 1947.

Stark, Benton. *The Year They Called Off the World Series: A True Story.* Garden City, New York: Avery Publishing Group, 1991.

Sullivan, Neil J. *The Dodgers Move West.* New York: Oxford University Press, 1987.

Thorn, John and John B. Holway. *The Pitcher.* Englewood Cliffs, New Jersey: Prentice-Hall and Company, 1987.

Tygiel, Jules. *Baseball's Great Experiment: Jackie Robinson and His Legacy.* New York: Oxford University Press, 1983 (New York: Vintage Books, 1984).

Wheeler, Lonnie and John Baskin. *The Cincinnati Game.* Wilmington, Ohio: Orange Frazer Press, 1988.

Zoss, Joel and John S. Bowman. *Diamonds in the Rough: The Untold History of Baseball.* New York: Collier Macmillan, 1989.

Sampler List of Outstanding Baseball Biographies

Aaron, Hank (with Lonnie Wheeler). *I Had a Hammer: The Hank Aaron Story.* New York: Harper Collins Publishers, 1991.

Alexander, Charles C. *Ty Cobb.* New York and London: Oxford University Press, 1984.

Alexander, Charles C. *John McGraw.* New York: Viking Penguin, 1988 (New York: Penguin Books, 1989).

Allen, Maury (with Bo Belinsky). *Bo—Pitching and Wooing.* New York: Dial Press, 1973.

Bartlett, Arthur. *Baseball and Mr. Spalding: The History and Romance of Baseball.* New York: Farrar, Straus and Young, 1951.

Campanella, Roy (with Joseph Reichler). *It's Good To Be Alive.* Boston: Little, Brown and Company, 1959.

Cepeda, Orlando (with Bob Markus). *High and Inside: Orlando Cepeda's Story.* South Bend, Indiana: Icarus Press, 1983.

Cobb, Ty (with Al Stump). *My Life in Baseball, The True Record.* New York: Doubleday and Company, 1961.

Creamer, Robert W. *Babe—The Legend Comes to Life.* New York: Simon and Schuster, 1974 (New York: Penguin Books, 1983).

Creamer, Robert W. *Stengel—His Life and Times.* New York: Simon and Schuster, 1984.

Durocher, Leo (with Ed Linn). *Nice Guys Finish Last.* New York: Simon and Schuster, 1975.

Durso, Joseph. *Casey and Mr. McGraw.* St. Louis, Missouri: The Sporting News, 1989.

Flood, Curt (with Richard Carter). *The Way It Is.* New York: Trident Press, 1971.

Greenberg, Hank (with Ira Berkow). *Hank Greenberg: The Story of My Life,* New York: Times Books, 1989.

Gropman, Donald. *Say It Ain't So, Joe! The Story of Shoeless Joe Jackson.* Boston: Little, Brown and Company, 1979 (New York: Lynx Books, 1988).

Hall, Donald (with Dock Ellis). *Dock Ellis and the Country of Baseball.* New York: Coward, McCann and Geoghegan, 1976 (New York: Simon and Schuster, 1989).

Higbe, Kirby (with Martin Quigley). *The High Hard One.* New York: The Viking Press, 1967.

Holway, John B. *Josh and Satch: The Life & Times of Josh Gibson and Satchel Paige.* Westport, Connecticut: Meckler Books, 1991, (New York: Carroll & Graf, 1992).

Kaufman, Louis, Barbara Fitzgerald, and Tom Sewell. *Moe Berg: Athlete, Scholar, Spy.* Boston: Little, Brown and Company, 1974.

Levine, Peter. *A.G. Spalding and the Rise of Baseball: The Promise of American Sport.* New York and London: Oxford University Press, 1985.

Lieb, Frederick G. *Baseball as I Have Known It.* New York: Coward, McCann and Geoghegan. 1977.

Mays, Willie (with Lou Sahadi). *Say Hey! The Autobiography of Willie Mays.* New York: Simon and Schuster, 1988.

Moore, Joseph Thomas. *A Pride Against Prejudice: The Biography of Larry Doby.* New York: Praeger Publishers, 1988.

Murdock, Eugene C. *Ban Johnson: Czar of Baseball.* Westport, Connecticut: Greenwood Press, 1982.

Musial, Stan (as told to Bob Broeg). *Stan Musial: The Man's Own Story.* Garden City, New York: Doubleday and Company, 1964.

Musick, Phil. *Who Was Roberto? Biography of Roberto Clemente.* Garden City, New York: Doubleday and Company, 1974.

Oh, Sadaharu, and David Falkner. *Sadaharu Oh: A Zen Way of Baseball.* New York: Times Books, 1984 (New York: Vintage Books, 1985).

Paige, LeRoy "Satchel" (as told to David Lipman). *Maybe I'll Pitch Forever: A Great Baseball Player Tells the Hilarious Story Behind the Legend.* Garden City, New York: Doubleday and Company, 1962.

Peterson, Harold. *The Man Who Invented Baseball (The Story of Alexander Cartwright).* New York: Charles Scribner's Sons, 1969.

Piersall, Jim, and Al Hirschberg. *Fear Strikes Out—The Jim Piersall Story.* Boston: Little, Brown and Company, 1955.

Polner, Murray. *Branch Rickey: A Biography.* New York: Atheneum Publishers, 1982.

Robinson, Jackie (as told to Alfred Duckett). *I Never Had It Made.* New York: G.P. Putnam's Sons, 1972.

Roseboro, John (with Bill Libby). *Glory Days with the Dodgers and Other Days with Others.* New York: Atheneum Publishers, 1978.

Smith, Curt. *America's Dizzy Dean.* St. Louis, Missouri: The Bethany Press, 1978.

Smith, Robert. *Babe Ruth's America.* New York: Thomas Y. Crowell Company, 1974.

Sobol, Ken. *Babe Ruth: The American Dream.* New York: Random House, 1974.
Veeck, Bill (with Ed Linn). *Veeck, As In Wreck: The Autobiography of Bill Veeck.* New York: G.P. Putnam's Sons, 1962.
Wagenheim, Kal. *Clemente!* New York: Praeger Publishers, 1973.
Wagenheim, Kal. *Babe Ruth: His Life and Times.* New York: Praeger Publishers, 1974 (Maplewood, New Jersey: Waterfront Press, 1990).
Williams, Ted (as told to John Underwood). *My Turn at Bat: The Story of My Life.* New York: Simon and Schuster, 1969.

Landmark Volumes on the History of Our National Pastime

Allen, Lee. *The American League Story.* New York: Hill and Wang, 1965.
Allen, Lee. *The National League Story.* New York: Hill and Wang, 1965.
Asinof, Eliot. *Eight Men Out: The Black Sox and the 1919 World Series.* New York: Holt, Rinehart and Winston, 1963 (New York: Henry Holt, 1987).
Bjarkman, Peter C. *The Brooklyn Dodgers.* New York: Chartwell Books, 1992.
Bjarkman, Peter C., ed. *Encyclopedia of Major League Baseball Team Histories: American League.* Westport, Connecticut: Meckler Books, 1991 (New York: Carroll & Graf, 1993).
Bjarkman, Peter C., ed. *Encyclopedia of Major League Baseball Team Histories: National League.* Westport, Connecticut: Meckler Books, 1991 (New York: Carroll & Graf, 1993).
Curran, William. *Big Sticks: The Batting Revolution of the Twenties.* New York: William Morrow Company, 1990 (New York: Harper Collins, 1991).
Dickey, Glenn. *The History of the World Series Since 1903.* New York: Stein and Day Publishers, 1984.

Fleming, G.H. *The Unforgettable Season (1908—The Most Exciting and Calamitous Pennant Race of All Time).* New York: Holt, Rinehart and Winston, 1981 (New York: Penguin Books, 1982).

Frommer, Harvey. *Primitive Baseball: The First Quarter-Century of the National Pastime.* New York: Atheneum, 1988.

Goldstein, Warren. *Playing for Keeps: A History of Early Baseball.* Ithaca and London: Cornell University Press, 1989.

Golenbock, Peter. *Bums: An Oral History of the Brooklyn Dodgers.* New York: G.P. Putnam's Sons, 1984.

Humber, William. *Cheering for Home Team: The Story of Baseball in Canada.* Erin, Ontario: The Boston Mills Press, 1983.

Leitner, Irving A. *Baseball: Diamond in the Rough.* New York and London: Criterion Books, 1972.

Lieb, Frederick G. *The Boston Red Sox.* New York: G.P. Putnam's Sons, 1947.

Linn, Ed. *The Great Rivalty—The Yankees and the Red Sox, 1901-1990.* New York: Ticknor and Field, 1991.

Luhrs, Victor. *The Great Baseball Mystery: The 1919 World Series.* New York: A.S. Barnes and Company, 1966.

Mann, Jack. *The Decline and Fall of the New York Yankees.* New York: Simon and Schuster, 1967.

Ritter, Lawrence, and Donald Honig. *The Image of Their Greatness: An Illustrated History of Baseball from 1900 to the Present.* New York: Crown Publishers, 1979.

Seymour, Harold. *Baseball: The Early Years.* New York: Oxford University Press, 1960.

Seymour, Harold. *Baseball: The Golden Age.* New York: Oxford University Press, 1971.

Shaughnessy, Dan. *The Curse of the Bambino.* New York: Dutton Publishers, 1990.

Smith, Robert. *World Series: The Games and the Players.* Garden City, New York: Doubleday and Company, 1967.

Sowell, Mike. *The Pitch That Killed—Carl Mays, Ray Chapman and the Pennant Race of 1920.* New York: Macmillan Publishing Company, 1989.

Voigt, David Q. *America Through Baseball.* Chicago: Nelson-Hall, 1976.

Wallop, Douglas. *Baseball: An Informal History.* New York: W.W. Norton and Company, 1969.

Dozen Best Books & Articles on Baseball's Mystical Numbers

Cook, Earnshaw. *Percentage Baseball.* Cambridge, Massachusetts: The M.I.T. Press, 1964.
Davids, L. Robert, ed. *Insider's Baseball—The Finer Points of the Game, as Examined by the Society for American Baseball Research.* New York: Charles Scribner's Sons, 1983.
Driscoll, David. *Blue Jays Jazz.* 1988 Edition. London, Ontario: Tag Communications, 1988.
Frolich, Cliff and Gary R. Scott. "Where Spectators Sit to Catch Baseballs" in: *Baseball Research Journal* 10 (1981), 132-138.
Gould, Stephen Jay. "Losing the Edge: The Extinction of the .400 Hitter" in: *Vanity Fair* (March 1983), 263-278.
James, Bill. *The Bill James Historical Baseball Abstract.* New York: Villard Books, 1986.
James, Bill. *This Time Let's Not Eat the Bones (Bill James Without the Numbers).* New York: Villard Books, 1989.
James, Bill, and John Dewan, eds. *Bill James Presents the Great American Baseball Stat Book.* New York: Ballantine Books, 1987.
Lane, F.C. "Why the System of Batting Averages Should be Changed" in: *The National Pastime: A Review of Baseball History* 6 (1987), 69-74. (a classic reprint, originally written in 1916)
Thorn, John, and Pete Palmer. *The Hidden Game of Baseball: A Revolutionary Approach to Baseball and Its Statistics.* Garden City, New York: Doubleday and Company, 1985.
Williams, Frank J. "All the Record Books are Wrong" in: *The National Pastime: A Review of Baseball History* 1 (1982), 50-62.
Wright, Craig R., and Tom House. *The Diamond Appraised.* New York: Simon and Schuster, 1989.

BASEBALL & THE GAME OF IDEAS

was typeset in 10 pt.

Palatino and printed on

80 lb. Mohawk vellum.